THE SHERLOCK HOLMES
IQ BOOK

THE SHERLOCK HOLMES

IQ BOOK

Being an Extract from the Reminiscences of John H. Watson, M.D., Late of the Army Medical Department

Puzzles supplied by Mensa

Eamonn Butler and Madsen Pirie

CARROLL & GRAF PUBLISHERS, INC.
NEW YORK

Copyright © 1995 by Eamonn Butler and Madsen Pirie

First Carroll & Graf edition 1996.

Carroll & Graf Publishers, Inc.
260 Fifth Avenue
New York, NY 10001

ISBN 0-7867-0330-X

Library of Congress Cataloging-in-Publication Data is available

Manufactured in the United States of America

CONTENTS

ACKNOWLEDGEMENTS

Special thanks are owed to our friends Harold Gale, the Executive Director of British Mensa, and Victor Serebriakoff, the President of Mensa. Thanks go also to all the Mensans who participated in devising and scoring these questions, and who helped with suggestions and advice.

Readers who are interested in joining Mensa, the high-IQ society, should write for details to Mensa, Freepost, Wolverhampton, United Kingdom.

We also acknowledge the use of the illustrations in this book, which are reproduced by kind permission of Westminster Libraries: the Sherlock Holmes Collection, Marylebone Library.

Dr Eamonn Butler
Dr Madsen Pirie

'The tin box I have lodged in the vaults of Cox & Co.'

FOREWORD

by Dr Eamonn Butler

One day, my uncle astonished me by mentioning that he had once had tea with Sir Arthur Conan Doyle. The orphaned Frank Butler was being raised by my great-aunt, Violet Ann Bland – twice imprisoned for the cause of Votes for Women, force-fed in prison, honoured by Mrs Pankhurst – at the guesthouse she ran in Old Burlington Street, London W.

There she would gather prominent supporters of the suffragette movement and quite naturally, one of these was Doyle, an ardent enthusiast of so many unrespectable causes.

Eagerly I pressed my uncle for details: What was the great man like? What did he say? What did he do?

'I don't really recall,' he replied. 'But I remember that he was a very *big* man.'

And that was it – all that he could tell me of the event!

What a disappointment: however, there must be few folk still alive who actually met this big man. And at least I can boast *some* direct family link with the reluctant creator of The Great Detective!

A NOTE ON SOURCES

by Dr Madsen Pirie

During recent building alterations near Trafalgar Square, a curious tin box came to light containing the notebooks, case-files and reminiscences of John H. Watson, MD, late of the Army Medical Department – apparently deposited there more than half a century ago when the building was the Charing Cross branch of Messrs Cox & Co, Bankers.

Knowing of our interest in the life and work of Mr Sherlock Holmes and his faithful colleague, these contents were very kindly made available to us, and form the basis of this publication.

However, much of the material discovered remains potentially embarrassing to the living relatives of certain individuals who featured (as clients or culprits) in Mr Holmes's investigations; and it is still doubtful that the world is yet prepared for the story of the *Matilda Briggs* and the giant rat of Sumatra. Accordingly, the box has been re-sealed and freshly deposited at another discreet location. The descendants of the politician involved in the affair of the lighthouse and the trained cormorant can rest easy for a few more years at least.

PREFACE:
HOW THIS
BOOK WORKS

by John H. Watson, M.D.,
Late of the Army Medical Department

Though many readers will be familiar with the fame of my distinguished friend, Mr Sherlock Holmes, from the stories that I have already published concerning his cases, comparatively few will know of the easy facility and amusement he had in both setting and answering puzzles and brain-teasers of every variety. So jealous was I to guard the professional reputation of my colleague that I excised from my writings any mention of this rather *infra dig* aspect of his personality.

Nevertheless, the time is fast approaching when Holmes's immortality is firmly guaranteed and when no such facts could ever dent it. So I have decided to flesh out a few of these little diversions that I recorded in my notebooks during our long partnership. These reflections I am depositing, with other files concerning the career of The Great Detective, in the tin box that I have lodged in the vaults of Cox & Co at Charing Cross, in the hope that they may be rediscovered and perhaps published when the time is right.

For each of the short stories that I have already laid before the public – and for two of the tales which were never finished to my satisfaction and so are not collected in the standard canon – I have detailed here one such example of this trivial intellectual amusement that we shared. For the longer tales, I have added four apiece.

I have collected the answers to these numerous riddles at the back of the book so that readers might pit their wits against The Great Detective – or, in a few cases, against my own humble self.

Occasionally, when framing a question, Holmes would indicate a certain time-limit of a few minutes. These limits I have recorded, so that those readers who allow themselves only a similar time to answer the relevant question can check to see whether or not they are up to the IQ figures quoted in the answers to those particular puzzles.

Where no time-limit is specified I suggest that readers allow themselves four minutes. I am sure that anyone able to solve most of these riddles in such a time would easily qualify to join Mensa, the high-IQ society.

Now, though, I must take my rest. I am by no means as sprightly as I once was, and the fragment of a Jezail bullet which I still carry is making its unwelcome presence all too painfully obvious.

The
Puzzles

A STUDY IN SCARLET

1. Mr Sherlock Holmes

*'The train of reasoning ran, "Here is a gentleman of a medical
type, but with the air of a military man. Clearly an army
doctor, then. He has just come from the tropics, for his face is
dark, and that is not the natural tint of his skin, for his wrists
are fair. He has undergone hardship and sickness, as his
haggard face says clearly. His left arm has been injured. He
holds it in a stiff and unnatural manner. Where in the tropics
could an English army doctor have seen so much hardship and
got his arm wounded? Clearly in Afghanistan." The whole
train of thought did not occupy a second.'*

THE FIRST account I wrote of Mr Sherlock Holmes and
his singular and remarkable methods was called A *Study
in Scarlet.*

In that narrative, I described not only how I was first
introduced to Holmes himself – and how he had almost
instantaneously deduced that I was an Army doctor who
had been wounded in Afghanistan – but also how I first
encountered the Scotland Yard detectives Lestrade and
Gregson, the inestimable Mrs Hudson, our long-suffering
landlady at 221B Baker Street, and the young Baker Street

Irregulars, whom Holmes at that time called his 'Street Arabs'.

The fellow who introduced us was young Stamford, once a dresser under me at Bart's. It had been a lucky encounter. I had arrived back in England, where I had neither kith nor kin, and was standing in solitary fashion at the Criterion Bar when Stamford tapped me on the shoulder. During our conversation I mentioned that I was looking for lodging; and so it was that he introduced me to Mr Sherlock Holmes, who required someone to share rooms in Baker Street.

I proposed a toast and told the barman to prepare an old regimental recipe which involved mixing four bottles of cider with one of wine. The barman informed me that the wine would cost twice as much per bottle as the cider. Stamford was still struggling to establish himself, and my wound pension had not yet come through, so we paid equal shares for our refreshment.

After much mental arithmetic – not helped by the grog – we worked out that the two of us should each pay seven and one-half pence to cover the cost of the concoction. It seemed a problem worthy of Holmes himself: How much, dear readers, do you suppose the wine cost?

2. The Lauriston Gardens Mystery

'Even across the street I could see a great blue anchor tattooed on the back of the fellow's hand. That smacked of the sea. He

had a military carriage, however, and regulation side-whiskers.
There we have the marine. He was a man with some amount
of self-importance and a certain air of command. You must
have observed the way in which he held his head and swung his
cane. A steady, respectable, middle-aged man too, on the face
of him – all facts which led me to believe that he had been a
sergeant.'
'Wonderful!' I ejaculated.
'Commonplace,' said Holmes.

I CAME TO know a great deal more about the character of Sherlock Holmes as we took up lodgings together in Baker Street, but it was on this, our first case together, that the enormous value of Holmes's very special talents was proved.

One morning – I have good reason to remember that it was the 4th of March – we were delivered a letter by the middle-aged man whom Holmes, gazing out of our first-floor window, had already pigeon-holed as a sergeant of Marines.

The letter was from Tobias Gregson of Scotland Yard. 'Gregson is the smartest of the Scotland Yarders,' explained Holmes. 'He and Lestrade are the pick of a bad lot.'

The Yard was asking for help in the case of the late Enoch J. Drebber, who had been found dead in an otherwise empty house at number 3, Lauriston Gardens, off the Brixton Road. There was no wound, yet there was blood everywhere – hence the title which I gave to my story.

At the scene of the crime Holmes carefully studied marks in the soil outside, quickly and expertly examined the corpse, and then spent twenty minutes or more in a painstaking examination of the room, using his pocket magnifying glass. It later transpired that this initial analysis had told Holmes virtually all the details of the case. A

'Come, Watson, come! The game is afoot!'

woman's ring was found at the scene, and the letters
RACHE written in blood upon the wall.

Lestrade had found the letters: the candle on the
mantelpiece had been lit at the time, making that the
brightest part of the room. Holmes examined the candle
and told me on the way home that it was of a very common
and very cheap type.

'One candle can be made from 7 candle stubs,' he told
me, 'and each candle gives 1 hour of light before it burns
to a stub.' His eyes twinkled as he tested me. 'So tell me,

Watson: If you have 98 of these candles, how many hours of light will it give you?'

'Not difficult,' I replied, 'though I shall need a piece of paper. The study of medicine took up the time which otherwise might have been spent on arithmetic.'

'Not remotely difficult, Watson,' he chided. 'You should be able to give me the correct answer within two minutes.'

I must be honest and confess that I could not.

3. Light in the Darkness

'I'll tell you one thing which may help you in the case,' he continued, turning to the two detectives. 'There has been murder done and the murderer was a man. He was more than six feet high, was in the prime of life, had small feet for his height, wore coarse, square-toed boots and smoked a Trichinopoly cigar. He came here with his victim in a four-wheeled cab, which was drawn by a horse with three old shoes and one new one on his off fore-leg. In all probability the murderer had a florid face, and the finger-nails of his right hand were remarkably long. These are only a few indications, but they may assist you.'

Lestrade and Gregson glanced at each other with an incredulous smile.

'If the man was murdered, how was it done?' asked the former.

'Poison,' said Sherlock curtly, and strode off.

WHILE THE Yard men pursued false leads – as in time I learned they invariably did – the deceased's secretary, one Joseph Strangerson, was found stabbed to death. The scene at his hotel was just as gruesome as that in Lauriston Gardens, with blood everywhere and again the blood-written letters RACHE on the wall.

Holmes not only solved the case at this point, identifying the culprit as Mr Jefferson Hope, but actually lured the suspect to our Baker Street rooms, and managed to handcuff the man in the presence of the two Scotland Yard detectives.

'What do you make of the letters RACHE?' I had asked him when we learnt of the hotel killing. 'You did not seem to think much of Lestrade's suggestion that it was intended to be the woman's name RACHEL, but was interrupted.'

'No,' said Holmes. 'As I said, it is German for revenge, and was a complete blind, designed to make us think of Socialism and secret societies.'

'But what does it mean?' I enquired.

'It means *red herring*,' said Holmes, amused at my baffled response to this. Then he gave me that quizzical look of his.

'Of course, Watson, if the word had been squared, I would have been more interested, and I would have suspected the involvement of a French priest.'

'Good Lord, Holmes!' I exclaimed. 'How could you possibly deduce such an unlikely thing?'

'Work it out for yourself, Watson,' he replied. Then he took out his pocket watch. 'It should take you no more than twelve minutes to tell me what kind of French priest.'

4. The Flower of Utah

*'Why, the height of a man, in nine cases out of ten, can be told
from the length of his stride. It is a simple calculation enough,
though there is no use my boring you with the figures. I had this
fellow's stride both on the clay outside and on the dust within.
Then I had a way of checking my calculation. When a man
writes on a wall, his instinct leads him to write above the level
of his own eyes. Now that writing was just over six feet from
the ground. It was child's play.'*

AFTER A violent struggle in which there was severe
bleeding from the culprit – I quickly diagnosed that
this, and his florid appearance, were due to an aortic
aneurism – Jefferson Hope was subdued, and then related
to us a saga of revenge which covered two continents and
the early history of the Mormon Church.

He recounted that the only survivors of a party crossing
the American West were John Ferrier and a girl called
Lucy, whom he later adopted. Saved by Mormons fleeing
persecution, they were required to join them.

When Salt Lake City and Utah were established, the
two prospered. As Lucy matured she met and fell in love
with Jefferson Hope, but the lovers were thwarted by
Mormon elders who wanted the girl for their vile polyga-
mous practices. Drebber and Strangerson killed John Ferrier and seized the girl. After she died, broken-hearted,
Jefferson Hope swore revenge, and years later, having
tracked his victims across America and Europe, took it in
London. But my companion in turn tracked him down by
his remarkable deductive methods.

Before a court appearance could be set, the Good Lord,

Whom I described as 'a higher Judge', took the matter in hand and Hope was found dead in his cell. I concluded my story by describing how Holmes and I read in the *Echo* about the 'triumph' and 'wonderful skills' of the Scotland Yard detectives.

One thing that powerfully impressed me about the case was the single-minded way in which Mr Jefferson Hope had pursued the miscreants through many of the major cities of America and Europe. I mentioned this to Holmes.

'Yes, the pursuit was remarkable for its intensity,' Holmes commented, 'and for the distances it covered.' He listed Salt Lake City, where it started, then Cleveland, St Petersburg, Paris, Copenhagen, and finally London.

'And there is one city I did not mention, Watson,' he added. 'It is 3,200 miles from Salt Lake City, 2,400 miles from Cleveland, 3,300 miles from St Petersburg, 1,300 miles from Paris, and 2,600 miles from Copenhagen.'

I cudgelled my brains, but could not work out where it was. 'I'm sorry, Holmes, but without an Atlas . . .'

'I do not want the name of the city, my friend, only its distance from London. And you will not need an Atlas. You should be able to work out the answer within, say, ten minutes.'

THE SIGN OF FOUR

5. The Science of Deduction

'Yes, I have been guilty of several monographs . . . Here, for example, is one "Upon the distinction between the Ashes of the Various Tobaccos". In it I enumerate a hundred and forty forms of cigar, cigarette, and pipe tobacco, with coloured plates illustrating the difference in the ash. It is a point which is continually turning up in criminal trials, and which is sometimes of supreme importance as a clue. If you can say definitely, for example, that some murder has been done by a man who was smoking an Indian lunkah, it obviously narrows your field of search. To the trained eye there is as much difference between the black ash of a Trichinopoly and the white fluff of bird's-eye as there is between a cabbage and a potato.'

ALTHOUGH SHERLOCK Holmes and I faced mortal peril as we unfolded the disturbing story of *The Sign of Four*, I will always be grateful that the case came our way. In the first place Holmes was locked into the ennui he called stagnation, and was resorting all too regularly to the cocaine bottle for his seven percent solution. The case provided him with a stimulus sharper than the drug and took him for a time away from the morbid process.

Holmes gave me four opportunities to test my own skills of reasoning and deduction during the course of our adventure, but I am afraid I was no match for the nimble brain and keen analytical insight of my companion. I pride myself none the less that I am in no sense inferior to Holmes in the human qualities which go to make for a successful and useful life. The fact that I was able to command the attention and respect of the lady who became my dear wife is some testament to that fact.

For *The Sign of Four* was the case that introduced me to that sweet lady, Miss Mary Morstan. This alone was worth any distress and any amount of danger, though we suspected neither when she first came to see us.

Her father had disappeared ten years ago on returning from India. In each of the past four years she had received an anonymous pearl of great value. Now a letter had asked her to bring two friends to a mysterious assignation that night.

Miss Morstan – and this case which would make such deep use of Sherlock Holmes's prodigious powers of deduction – came to us just as I had been trying to nudge The Great Detective out of his intellectual torpor by entreating him to explain the elements of that remarkable science.

'The science of deduction requires its practitioner, among other things, to notice connections,' he explained. 'One has to see the relations between things which appear, to the untrained eye, to be unrelated.'

He scribbled five words on a scrap of paper and handed it to me. On the paper was written:

COMPOTE   SCUPPER   SPANIEL

FEWER   RETINUE

'This is altogether too trivial and mundane to be of any interest, except as an example of the point,' he continued. 'Of course, you perceive the relationship between the five words. You see instantly what it is they have in common.' And he gazed in a bored manner out into the swirling fog.

Within five minutes, I did manage to find the connection. By that time my friend was almost completely submerged in his own languid introspections.

6. The Tragedy of Pondicherry Lodge

'It is very customary for pawnbrokers in England, when they take a watch, to scratch the numbers of the ticket with a pin-point upon the inside of the case. It is more handy than a label as there is no risk of the number being lost or transposed. There are no less than four such numbers visible to my lens on the inside of this case. Inference – that your brother was often at low water. Secondary inference – that he had occasional bursts of prosperity, or he could not have redeemed the pledge. Finally, I will ask you to look at the inner plate, which contains the keyhole. Look at the thousands of scratches all round the hole – marks where the key has slipped. What sober man's key could have scored those grooves? But you will never see a drunkard's watch without them. He winds it at night, and he

*leaves these traces of his unsteady hand. Where is the mystery
in all this?'*

O F COURSE Holmes and I agreed to go with Miss
Morstan, and we were all driven to a house on the
south side of the river. There we met Thaddeus Sholto,
who told Miss Morstan that her father had been a colleague
of his father, Major Sholto, but had collapsed and died in
his presence ten years ago. The Major told his sons of a
vast treasure, but died himself after a hideous face appeared
at the window. The next morning the sons had found their
father's room rifled, and a scrap of paper bearing the legend
'The Sign of Four'.

One of the brothers, Bartholomew, had discovered the
treasure in an attic cubicle, and it was from this that Miss
Morstan had received her yearly pearl.

We all drove to Pondicherry Lodge, where Bartholomew
lived, to settle the matter, but found Bartholomew dead,
his face and limbs twisted and distorted, and the treasure
gone. Holmes ascertained that he had been poisoned by a
tipped thorn, and that a child-sized creature had climbed
up and entered via the attic, lowering a rope for his
wooden-legged companion to join him.

Already, Holmes's mind was racing ahead. 'You must
enjoy manipulating words, Watson,' he told me.

'Since you know how I write about your cases, Holmes,
that is not a difficult deduction,' I replied, smugly.

'Then let me tell you that the man with a wooden leg
we seek is short, and his name is Small. Now, Watson,
take me from SHORT to SMALL in five stages, changing
only one letter at a time, and forming a complete English
word with every move. Tell me the intermediate words. I
will allow you ten minutes while I check for any further
clues here.'

With that, Holmes took my pocket watch, flipped it open and began to time me.

7. Sherlock Holmes Gives a Demonstration

'His name, I have every reason to believe, is Jonathan Small. He is a poorly educated man, small, active, with his right leg off, and wearing a wooden stump which is worn away on the inner side. His left boot has a coarse, square-toed sole, with an iron band around the heel. He is a middle-aged man, much sunburned, and has been a convict. These few indications may be of some assistance to you, coupled with the fact that there is a good deal of skin missing from the palm of his hand.'

I WAS completely flummoxed by these nefarious and dark circumstances, but Holmes took it all in his stride. After much measuring and examining, he cried with delight when he saw that the small and agile one had stepped in some creosote. Even as Scotland Yard's representative, Mr Athelney Jones, appeared at the scene to make wrong suppositions and to arrest practically everyone in sight, Holmes sent me to an address in Pinchin Lane to borrow a dog called Toby to aid our pursuit.

Toby had as good a nose as Holmes had told me, and led us across London on the trail of the creosote scent. Despite the false lead of a barrel of the stuff, he did track the suspects to a wharf, where we discovered they had hired a fast steamboat called the *Aurora*. We then faced

15

'What do you make of that?'

more than a day of irritation as the best efforts of Holmes's 'Street Arabs' and a newspaper advertisement failed to produce the whereabouts of the *Aurora*. Holmes, however, in a brilliant seafaring disguise which fooled myself and Athelney Jones, had found out from where she was to leave that night.

In *A Study in Scarlet* I mentioned how astonished I was to discover Holmes ignorant of the Copernican Theory, and that he did not know that the earth and other planets revolved around the sun. When I told him he replied that he would do his best to forget it, since it was of not the remotest importance in his work.

Obviously he had not done so, however. For while we were passing time waiting for news from the Baker Street Irregulars, he set me the following problem.

'I think you might find this little enigma not entirely devoid of interest, Watson,' said he. 'If one planet revolves clockwise around the sun every 7 years, and another one does so in 56 years, and they both start in line on the same side of the sun, how long will it be before the sun and those two planets are next in a straight line?'

He gave me fifteen minutes to work out the answer, but I do not think I could have done it in fifteen days!

8. The End of the Islander

'The division seems rather unfair,' I remarked. 'You have done all the work in this business. I get a wife out of it, Jones gets the credit, pray what remains for you?'
'For me,' said Sherlock Holmes, 'there remains the cocaine-bottle.' And he stretched his long white hand up for it.

IN ONE of the most thrilling chases I have ever been engaged upon, we pursued the *Aurora* in a fast police launch. As we gained on her, we saw on deck the one-legged man and his mysterious companion whom Holmes had identified as a savage from the Andaman Isles. As the savage raised his blowpipe, Holmes and I both fired and saw him fall overboard. Wooden-leg, identified by Holmes as Jonathan Small, was trapped in the mud and taken into custody, together with the treasure chest.

We were disappointed to find the chest empty when we later opened it. Jonathan Small told us he had dumped the treasure in the Thames, rather than allow it to fall into the wrong hands. He then told us his amazing story, most of which my companion, by a dazzling exercise of his great gift, had already deduced. It was a chilling tale of greed, murder and retribution which had begun in India.

Jonathan Small, with three Indian accomplices, had murdered a merchant for his treasure at the time of the mutiny. They swore a sacred oath to each other, buried the treasure, and each received a map of its location bearing the sign of the four of them.

Condemned to a prison island for the murder, but with the treasure still buried, Small struck a deal with two of the guards, Morstan and Sholto. Sholto took the treasure and reneged on the deal. Morstan had died on the night he returned to England, leaving an embittered Small to break free of prison and come, with his Andaman native accomplice, to seek the treasure and take revenge.

Small would have succeeded, but it was his misfortune to come up against the sharpest mind in all England; that of my celebrated friend, who outwitted him and matched him in cunning and daring.

When our speculations had turned to the Andaman Islands and to the curious inhabitant armed with his deadly thorns, Holmes read me the entry about the Andamans from the first volume of his gazetteer. Then he looked up other entries and began to scribble a drawing, which he handed to me.

'What do you make of that, Watson?' he asked.

'It is encrypted,' I replied, 'and it concerns geographical places.'

'Excellent!' laughed Holmes. 'What you must do, my friend, is to rearrange each group of letters to spell out in each row of boxes an island chain. Then take the letters indicated by the shaded text and rearrange them to make a fifth island chain.'

'It *does* look rather difficult, Holmes.'

'Pshaw, my dear fellow. Given all that I have already taught you concerning the subtle science of deduction, I shall indeed be disappointed in you if you cannot give me the answer to such a trifle within eight minutes.'

This was the drawing he had given me:

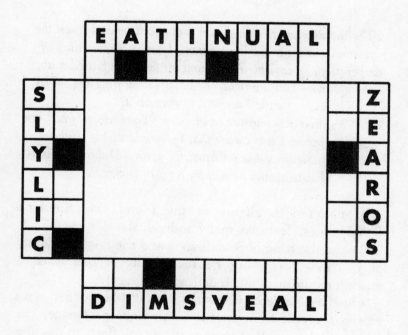

THE ADVENTURES OF SHERLOCK HOLMES

9. A Scandal in Bohemia

The man sprang from his chair and paced up and down the room in uncontrollable agitation. Then, with a gesture of desperation, he tore the mask from his face and hurled it upon the ground. 'You are right,' he cried; 'I am the King. Why should I attempt to conceal it?'

'Why, indeed?' murmured Holmes. 'Your Majesty had not spoken before I was aware that I was addressing Wilhelm Gottsreich Sigismond von Ormstein, Grand Duke of Cassel-Felstein, and hereditary King of Bohemia.'

AMONG THE clients of my friend, Mr Sherlock Holmes, featured many individuals of royal blood, including the King of Scandinavia and the reigning family of Holland (for whom he successfully accomplished a mission requiring of much delicacy and tact).

One day – indeed, it was the 20th of March 1888 – we received a visit from another such royal personage, the King of Bohemia, that same man whose efforts to disguise his identity survived scarcely a moment under the withering scrutiny of Holmes's remarkable powers of observation and deduction.

The King had good reasons for demanding discretion. The task he set for my friend was to recover a photograph of himself and Miss Irene Adler, a former opera singer, which he believed might be used to compromise him.

It was one of those rare cases where Holmes found himself beaten – or at least matched. He quickly discovered where in Miss Adler's house the embarrassing picture was located; though in the end she was sharp enough to anticipate his next move and escape with it.

I had arranged to meet Holmes in Baker Street at three o'clock on the afternoon after the King's appearance. Holmes himself was out collecting information on Miss Adler and her household – so in fact it was close upon four before he returned, in a disguise of his own.

Meanwhile, I settled down to read the *Evening News* for a time, until I discovered one of the little conundrums which he would often dash off for his own amusement and leave thoughtlessly on the table, or mixed up with his correspondence, transfixed by a jack-knife on the very centre of the mantelpiece.

This particular one he had rolled up and used as a taper to light one of his foul pipes, so the place where he had written the solution was charred away. I fevered to work out the answer to the puzzle. Here is how it ran:

Question: what do these strange words have in common?

GROAN   TRILANCE

ROBOTMEN   HONEYPLOX

10. The Red-headed League

Sherlock Holmes's quick eye took in my occupation, and he shook his head with a smile as he noticed my questioning glances. 'Beyond the obvious facts that he has at some time done manual labour, that he takes snuff, that he is a Freemason, that he has been in China, and that he has done a considerable amount of writing lately, I can deduce nothing else.'

THE RED-HEADED League was a most curious institution. We were introduced to it by Mr Jabez Wilson, the pawnbroker whose travels, tobacco addiction, and other personal details so quickly revealed themselves to the scrutiny of Mr Sherlock Holmes, and who came to Baker Street one October day in 1890 to consult my good friend over its strange activities.

Mr Wilson, who himself had a full head of red hair of the most fiery shade, had been surprised to find himself accepted by the League at a wage of four sovereigns per week – for doing no more than copying out the *Encyclopaedia Britannica*.

Our client was even more distressed when, a few weeks later, he attended the same offices at the usual hour, only to find the door locked and a notice posted to say that the Red-headed League was now dissolved.

Holmes quickly reasoned that the League was no more than a ruse to distract Mr Wilson while some serious crime was being contemplated and executed. He informed me of this last conclusion, and asked me to meet him again at ten o'clock on what could turn out to be a mission of some little danger.

As I drove home to my house in Kensington I thought over the whole case, trying to puzzle out everything that Holmes had already concluded from the red-headed copier of the *Encyclopaedia* and our visits to his business premises earlier in the day. Though I tried hard to fit the facts into some coherent theory, I could not make any explanation work.

So gradually, as the hansom made its way across London, I found my mind wandering on to a slightly less difficult sort of problem. It was in my pocket: one of those little diversions which my friend Holmes would scribble down and leave lying around, and which I had gathered up in the hope of solving when I had the time.

I wished that I had the *Encyclopaedia* with me, because it seemed to be a very strange word that he had scrawled in his familiar hand. Or was it some coded note from a person with an extraordinarily long and strange name?

Three household items [it ran]:

CCCONAORKKETSSACITREANWERND

11. A Case of Identity

'Do you not find,' he said, 'that with your short sight it is a little trying to do so much typewriting?'
'I did at first,' she answered, 'but now I know where the letters are without looking.' Then, suddenly realizing the full

purport of his words, she gave a violent start and looked up,
with fear and astonishment upon her broad, good-humoured
face. 'You've heard about me, Mr Holmes,' she cried, 'else
how could you know all that?'
'Never mind,' said Holmes, laughing. 'It is my business to
know things. Perhaps I have trained myself to see what others
overlook.'

MISS MARY Sutherland was the name of the short-sighted typist who consulted us in Baker Street concerning the disappearance of her fiancé, Mr Hosmer Angel.

She had met him at the gasfitters' ball, and became engaged to him after the first walk they took together. She knew that her stepfather, Mr James Windibank, would oppose any match; but with the consent and encouragement of Miss Sutherland's mother, they arranged to marry within the week.

You can imagine Miss Sutherland's disappointment when, on her wedding morning, her fiancé did not appear – despite the testimony of the cabman that he had certainly seen him get into the four-wheeler and could not imagine what had happened to him.

Holmes listened to her story. 'I shall write two letters,' he said to me, 'which should settle the matter.'

By this time I had so many reasons to believe in my friend's subtle powers of deduction that I felt he must have some solid grounds for the assured and easy manner in which he seemed to think that this singular mystery could be so easily solved.

'And now, Doctor,' he continued, 'we can do nothing until the answers to those letters come, so we may put our little problem upon the shelf for the interim. But let me divert you for a few minutes with a less profound little mystery which came to me earlier today.

'I myself attended the gasfitters' ball some years ago. No, Watson, it is *not* my preferred sort of social gathering, of course not – but I had to don the appropriate disguise and observe some of the guests at this annual function when I was clearing up the singular tragedy of the Atkinson brothers.

'Gasfitters,' he went on, 'apparently consume quite a staggering volume of beer at this occasion. One of my acquaintances, Charlie, drank 10 pints more than another, Spike, who in turn drank 7 pints less than Tom. Spike and Brian drank 8 pints between them. Brian drank 2 more than Mick, but Tom drank 3 more than Brian. Quite a total, eh, Watson?'

'But what *was* the total?' I enquired.

'Really, Watson, I have given you all the information you need to work it out for yourself. If you cannot compute that simple figure in five minutes, I shall have to pronounce you dull indeed!'

12. The Boscombe Valley Mystery

'And the murderer?'
'Is a tall man, left-handed, limps with the right leg, wears thick-soled shooting-boots and a gray cloak, smokes Indian cigars, uses a cigar-holder, and carries a blunt pen-knife in his pocket. There are several other indications, but these may be enough to aid us in our search.'

ON MONDAY, June 3rd, Mr Charles McCarthy, an ex-Australian, left his house at Hatherley in Hereford-shire, and walked down towards the Boscombe Pool. Witnesses saw him near the lake, engaged in a violent argument with his son James. A few minutes later, James

'We had the carriage to ourselves.'

arrived at the lodge in an agitated state, his right hand and sleeve stained with fresh blood; while his father's body was found at the lakeside, his head beaten in by repeated blows of some heavy and blunt weapon – like the butt-end of James's gun.

I could hardly have imagined a more damning case. But Holmes appeared unconvinced. On his telegram summons, I joined him on the 11.15 from Paddington, and we made our way up to Herefordshire.

We lunched at Swindon. 'You may have noticed that four different spices have been used in the preparation of our meal today, Watson,' laughed Holmes as we sat to digest our brief repast. 'And I observe that, if you mix up the letters of their names you can produce the line CUNNING MEN ARE DOING MORE TRACING.

'Can you tell me what the spices in question might be? Think quickly, now – we have only twelve minutes to catch our connecting train!'

13. The Five Orange Pips

Sherlock Holmes sat for some time in silence, with his head sunk forward and his eyes bent upon the red glow of the fire. Then he lit his pipe, and leaning back in his chair he watched the blue smoke-rings as they chased each other up to the ceiling.
'I think, Watson,' he remarked at last, 'that of all our cases we have had none more fantastic than this.'

THE YEAR '87 furnished us with a long list of cases, but none of them presented such singular features as the train of circumstances which Mr John Openshaw reported to us that September.

On 10 March 1883, he recounted, his uncle Elias had received a letter with a foreign stamp. All the envelope contained was five little dried orange pips, though this seemed to give his uncle some strange foreboding of death. And true enough, just a few weeks later, on 2nd May, he was found dead at the foot of the garden.

But this was not the only victim. In January 1885, Mr Openshaw's father received a message of the same sort; and he too was found dead within the month.

And now, five orange pips had been delivered to Mr Openshaw himself. Having been laughed off by the official police, it was perhaps no wonder that he braved the equinoctal gales (which were of exceptional violence that year) to seek the advice of Mr Sherlock Holmes.

Holmes analysed the facts of the case and directed Mr Openshaw to return home immediately and take the action which he deduced would end the threat to his person – placing the contents of a certain box on his garden sundial.

'I believe the only chance young Openshaw has is to do what I have told him,' he remarked, as the wind and the rain lashed at our shutters. 'There is nothing more to be said or done tonight, so hand me over my violin and let us try to forget for half an hour the miserable weather and the still more miserable ways of our fellowmen.'

I have to say that, although Holmes was accomplished at the violin, his nocturnal scrapings tended often to have an extemporaneous *ad lib* quality that sometimes strayed quite far from the accepted notions of melody. Fearing that tonight might be no different from usual, I sought to distract him.

'This sundial thing makes me think,' said I. 'I started musing about the sun, the moon, and the stars; and I wonder how many moves it would take to change the word MOON into STAR, changing only one letter at a time such that all the intervening steps formed meaningful words? Seven or eight, perhaps . . . ?'

'Five steps – that is to say, four intermediate words – would be quite sufficient,' my friend cut in, without raising his eyes from the strings of his violin. 'Surely that's obvious, Watson?'

'I'm sure it is,' I replied: and I knitted my brow and tried to reason out what he had seen in an instant. His eccentric and spirited violin playing hardly helped me in this effort.

14. The Man with the Twisted Lip

'I perceive also that whoever addressed the envelope had to go and inquire as to the address.'
'How can you tell that?'
'The name, you see, is in perfectly black ink, which has dried itself. The rest is of the grayish colour, which shows that blotting-paper has been used. If it had been written straight off, and then blotted, none would be of a deep black shade. This man has written the name, and there has then been a pause before he wrote the address, which can only mean that he was not familiar with it. It is, of course, a trifle, but there is nothing so important as trifles.'

HOLMES AND I were staying at The Cedars, near Lee in Kent, the home of Mrs Neville St Clair. Her husband had mysteriously disappeared; and although he was the very embodiment of a respectable moneyed gentleman, he had last been spotted in one of the vilest areas of London, in the upper window of a notorious opium den.

Not having much else to go on, Inspector Bradstreet of Bow Street police station decided to hold one Hugh Boone, a crippled beggar with a disfigured face and a shock of orange hair, who was the last person to have seen Mr St Clair alive.

Mrs St Clair welcomed us with great hospitality, considering the troubles she was then enduring, and put two rooms at our disposal. After a night thinking out the problem (and consuming an ounce of shag in the process) Holmes announced to me that he must have been 'one of the most absolute fools in Europe', that he deserved 'to be kicked from here to Charing Cross', and that the key to the affair was in the bathroom!

I was astonished by such ejaculations, but I had more than sufficient confidence in my friend's uncommon powers to accept that, remarkable though it be, he probably had indeed found some sort of key that would unlock the mystery.

As we dashed down the London Road in our horse and trap, Holmes displayed that easy confidence which came to him when he knew that he had the right solution to a difficult problem. 'It has been in some points a singular case,' said he. 'I confess that I have been as blind as a mole, but it is better to learn wisdom late than never to learn it at all.'

At such moments, he was quite capable of letting his mind free to dart off into flights of fancy, and given the length of the drive, he had obviously decided to amuse himself for a few minutes at my expense.

'Now that I have solved my puzzle, Watson,' he continued, 'let me pose another for you to trifle with. You may have noticed that the taps in the bathroom were not exactly matched in terms of their rate of output.'

'I cannot say I had really noticed, Holmes.'

'As I have observed to you many times, my dear friend, many issues of crucial importance can hang on the observation of such seemingly trivial details. But to continue: by my watch, the hot tap filled the bath in 16 minutes . . .'

'When the plug was in, I presume.'

'Quite so, when the bath was plugged. The cold tap, however, ran a little more quickly, and took only 15 minutes to fill the bath – when the plug was in. Now, I observed that the full bath, with the taps off and the plug taken out, drained dry in precisely 14 minutes. So tell me, how long – to the nearest second will do – would it take to fill the bath with the plug *out* and both taps running?'

'We will reach Bow Street in ten minutes, Watson. Let's see if you can work it out in that time.'

15. The Blue Carbuncle

*'Then, pray tell me what it is that you can infer from this hat?'
He picked it up and gazed at it in the peculiar introspective
fashion which was characteristic of him. 'It is perhaps less
suggestive than it might have been,' he remarked, 'and yet there
are a few inferences which are very distinct, and a few others*

which represent at least a strong balance of probability. That
the man was highly intellectual is of course obvious upon the
face of it, and also that he was fairly well-to-do within the last
three years, although he has now fallen upon evil days. He had
foresight, but has less now than formerly, pointing to a moral
retrogression, which, when taken with the decline in his
fortunes, seems to indicate some evil influence, probably drink,
at work upon him. This may account also for the obvious fact
that his wife has ceased to love him.'

'My dear Holmes!'

'He has, however, retained some degree of self-respect,' he
continued, disregarding my remonstrance. 'He is a man who
leads a sedentary life, goes out little, is out of training entirely,
is middle-aged, has grizzled hair which he has had cut within the
last few days, and which he anoints with lime-cream. These are
the more patent facts which are to be deduced from his hat.
Also, by the way, that it is extremely improbable that he has
gas laid on in his house.'

EARLY ONE Christmas morning, Peterson, the commissionaire, stumbled across an argument between a tall man, who was carrying a goose, and a little knot of roughs. The appearance of his uniformed figure startled the combatants, and the tall man dropped his goose – and the hat which told Holmes so much about the man's character and family circumstances – and vanished into the streets.

Having asked Holmes's advice, Peterson took the goose home to be cooked. But he and his wife were even more astonished to find in its crop a brilliantly scintillating stone – which Holmes instantly identified as the Countess of Morcar's blue carbuncle diamond.

He sent Peterson out to place an advertisement in the London evening papers – 'in the *Globe, Star, Pall Mall, St James's, Evening News, Standard, Echo,* and any others that occur to you' – which he thought would help bring a speedy resolution to the mystery. Nothing more could be done, he told me, until that advertisement was answered.

I had my professional round to get on with, but I stayed on for a few minutes, just enough time for Holmes to see if my mental abilities were up to another of his little problems.

'Here's a seasonal question for you, Watson,' said he, handing over a scribbled diagram.

'Now, when completed, no row, column or diagonal will use the same letter of the word FROST more than once. What letter will appear in the bottom left-hand corner, where the question mark is located at present?'

I looked at Holmes's scribble, weighing up whether I really had time to puzzle it out, or whether I should be getting on with my round and attending to this when I had more time. After a few moments in thought, however, the solution came to me easily enough.

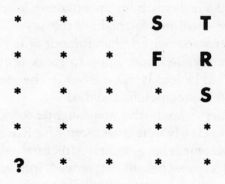

16. The Speckled Band

'You have come in by train this morning, I see.'
'You know me, then?'
'No, but I observe the second half of a return ticket in the palm of your left glove. You must have started early, and yet you had a good drive in a dog-cart, along heavy roads, before you reached the station.'
The lady gave a violent start and stared in bewilderment at my companion.
'There is no mystery, my dear madam,' said he, smiling.

I CANNOT recall a case which presented more singular features than that which came to us in April '83, concerning the well-known family of the Roylotts of Stoke Moran, on the western border of Surrey.

Miss Helen Stoner, the client who rose so early to consult The Great Detective, reported that her sister had suffered sudden death from an unknown cause some two years earlier – within a fortnight of the day which had been fixed for her wedding. She had run out of her room, limbs dreadfully convulsed, managing to speak only the words, 'Oh, my God! Helen! It was the band! The speckled band!' before she fell unconscious and died.

Now Miss Stoner, the stepdaughter of Dr Grimesby Roylott, was clearly in fear and terror for her own life. She too had become engaged; and structural repairs at the house had caused her to be moved into the self-same bedroom in which her sister had met her dreadful fate.

Holmes and I travelled down to Stoke Moran. We had no difficulty in engaging a bedroom and sitting-room at the Crown Inn, from which we could command a view of the avenue gate, and of the inhabited wing of that decaying hulk, Stoke Moran Manor House.

As we waited for darkness to descend, so that Holmes and I could start to work on his clandestine plan that would eventually produce a solution to the mystery, we took a light dinner in our room, during which Holmes put to me the following conundrum that perhaps revealed his suspicions.

'Still ten minutes of light left, Watson,' he said, peering through the gap he had left in the drawn curtains. 'In that time you should be able to solve this little poser.' And he scribbled the following words on a leaf from his pocket-book:

TART (　　) THEM
SHELL (　　) CLAIM
CART (　　) RUSH
PAN (　　) RED

'Now, two letters, placed inside each set of brackets, will create other words when added to the end of the word to the left and the beginning of the word to the right. When completed, another word can be read downwards. What is the word?'

17. The Engineer's Thumb

*'He drew up the windows on either side, tapped on the wood-
work, and away we went as fast as the horse could go.'*
'One horse?' interjected Holmes.
'Yes, only one.'
'Did you observe the colour?'
*'Yes, I saw it by the side-lights when I was stepping into the
carriage. It was a chestnut.'*
'Tired-looking, or fresh?'
'Oh, fresh and glossy.'
*'Thank you. I am sorry to have interrupted you. Pray
continue your most interesting statement.'*

VICTOR HATHERLEY, a hydraulic engineer with a
struggling practice on the third floor of 16A Victoria
Street, arrived in my consulting-room early one morning
with a gruesome injury. It was one such as gave even my
hardened nerves a shudder to look at it – he had lost his
thumb, which had been hacked or torn right out from the
roots.

On learning that this was no mere accident but a
murderous attack, I recommended he accompany me to my
friend Mr Sherlock Holmes.

At Baker Street we found Holmes, as I expected,
lounging about the sitting-room in his dressing-gown,
reading the agony column of *The Times* and smoking his
before-breakfast pipe. Mr Hatherley reported how he had
been lured out, late at night, to examine a mechanical
failure in a large hydraulic press at some secret location.

36

He had been met at Eyford station by a carriage, but since it had frosted-glass windows and the night was dark, he was unable to say precisely where he was taken.

After inspecting the machinery he luckily survived an attack upon his life, but lost a thumb in making his escape. So what was it that was so secret, and which prompted his attempted murder?

To Holmes, with his faithful Index, the case was a repeat of an earlier disappearance of a hydraulic engineer, and he quickly pin-pointed the location of the crime, and its explanation.

As the three of us travelled down by train to Eyford, in the presence of Inspector Bradstreet of Scotland Yard and a plain-clothes man, my friend – already confident that he had done all the intellectual work necessary to solve the mystery – amused us by asking the engineer an interesting question.

'Here's a problem that an engineer should be able to solve quickly enough, Hatherley. Four cog wheels are in a mesh. The largest has 102 teeth, the next 54, the next 32 and the smallest 24. Got that? Good! Now the cogs begin to revolve. How many revolutions will the largest cog make before they are back to the start position?'

18. The Noble Bachelor

'Who ever heard of such a mixed affair? Every clue seems to slip through my fingers. I have been at work upon it all day.'
'And very wet it seems to have made you,' said Holmes, laying his hand upon the arm of the pea-jacket.

'Yes, I have been dragging the Serpentine.'
'In heaven's name, what for?'
'In search of the body of Lady St Simon.'
Sherlock Holmes leaned back in his chair and laughed
heartily.
'Have you dragged the basin of Trafalgar Square fountain?'
he asked.
'Why? What do you mean?'
'Because you have just as good a chance of finding this lady
in the one as in the other.'
Lestrade shot an angry glance at my companion. 'I suppose
you know all about it,' he snarled.
'Well, I have only just heard the facts, but my mind is
made up.'

LORD ST Simon – the second son of the Duke of Balmoral – asked for the help of Sherlock Holmes when his new bride, the former Miss Hatty Doran of San Francisco, mysteriously left the wedding breakfast and disappeared.

The police arrested Miss Flora Millar, who had caused some little trouble by attempting to force her way into the house where the bridal party were celebrating, alleging that she had some prior claim on Lord St Simon.

A vital clue – an enigmatic note written on the back of a hotel bill – had implicated Miss Millar, a former *danseuse* at the Allegro, who had known the bridegroom for some years.

To Inspector Lestrade of Scotland Yard, this clue suggested a case of abduction and murder, prompting him to drag the lake near the scene of the disappearance. But to Mr Sherlock Holmes, the clue recommended an alternative course of action which revealed that a very different sort of tragedy had occurred.

With the case solved, and supper taken, Holmes and I could relax. 'Draw your chair up and hand me my violin,' said he, 'for the only problem we have still to solve is how to while away these bleak autumnal evenings.' However, I was sufficiently hesitant to subject myself, after so satisfying a supper, to another of his eccentric *ad lib* compositions, that again I attempted to divert his mind on to something different.

'Supposing that Miss Doran had received a cheque on which, by mistake, the dollars had been transposed for cents and vice versa,' said I, thinking as quickly as I could. 'If she spent $5.22 and found that she had in change exactly 28 times the value of the original cheque, what *ought* she to have received?'

'The calculation is a simple one,' retorted my friend. And he gave me the answer and carried on with his discordant scraping.

19. The Beryl Coronet

'It is an old maxim of mine that when you have excluded the impossible, whatever remains, however improbable, must be the truth.'

MR ALEXANDER Holder, senior partner in the City of London's second largest banking concern of Holder & Stevenson, called upon us one wintry morning in a state of considerable agitation.

He recounted the most astonishing tale of misfortune. It seems that he had advanced a short-term loan of £50,000 to a prominent client – indeed, it was to one of the highest, noblest, and most exalted persons in England – taking as security the famous Beryl Coronet.

Of course, this jewel was among the most precious public possessions of the Empire. And fearing for its safety, Mr Holder decided not to lock it in the bank's own safe but to carry it with him at all times. He called a cab to his home in Streatham and locked it in his dressing-room bureau.

That night, however, he was awakened by some sound in the house, and heard footsteps in his dressing-room. Fearfully peeping round the door, he was astonished and alarmed to see his wayward son, Arthur, grasping the Coronet, which had been broken, with three of its stones missing.

By analysing the tracks that were still visible in the snow around the house, Holmes was able to find the missing fragment and elicit a full explanation of the extraordinary events that had unfolded at the unfortunate banker's residence.

I saw all this first-hand, because Holmes insisted on me accompanying him on this expedition to Streatham, though for most of the journey he sat silently in thought. The distressed and agitated banker, though, appeared to have taken fresh heart from my famous friend's interest in the case, and even broke into a desultory chat with me over his business affairs. I did my best to reassure our client of Holmes's extraordinary powers – citing how he had unravelled similar mysteries both in the case of Mrs Farintosh and the opal tiara (although that was a bit before my time), and in the Armsworth Castle business.

Eventually he cheered up even further. 'This cold weather reminds me of a little puzzle that one of the clerks at Holder & Stevenson put to me a while ago,' said he.

'Indeed, I wonder what your distinguished colleague would make of this. What you have to do is complete this square so that three more words can be read downwards and across, using 2 Es, 2 Gs, 2 Hs, I, R and Y. What are the words?'

And he wrote out the word-square, thus:

20. The Copper Beeches

'Pshaw, my dear fellow, what do the public, the great unobservant public, who could hardly tell a weaver by his tooth or a compositor by his left thumb, care about the finer shades of analysis and deduction! But indeed, if you are trivial, I cannot blame you, for the days of the great cases are past. Man, or at least criminal man, has lost all enterprise and originality.'

THOUGH SHERLOCK Holmes was beginning to fear that his agency had reached its low point, the thick fog of early spring brought us at least one criminal investigation worthy of his talents – the curious occurrences which took place at The Copper Beeches, five miles on the far side of Winchester.

Miss Violet Hunter had been engaged as a governess by Mr and Mrs Jephro Rucastle – and at around three times the normal rate for the work. But he had alarmed her by suggesting, on their first interview, that if she accepted the position she might be required to cut her luxuriant hair and, on occasion, to sit in a particular place and wear a particular dress of the Rucastles' choice.

On hearing her story, Holmes immediately sensed that Miss Hunter was in some danger, and in response to her urgent summons a fortnight later, we made our way to the old English capital.

Over lunch at the Black Swan Hotel, Miss Hunter told us more of the extraordinary goings-on at The Copper Beeches, which seemed to confirm Holmes's suspicions. He decided on taking action when the time was right.

'We can do nothing until seven o'clock,' said he, once he had heard her full story. 'At that hour we shall be with you, and it will not be long before we solve the mystery.'

So we put up our trap at a wayside public house, and, finding that we had the best part of an afternoon and early evening to while away, we fell amicably into toying with some rather less sinister little mysteries.

'A seasonal riddle, for you, Watson!' said Holmes. 'These six words have a connection. What is it?'

The words were:

VISIT   APPLE   CARAT

SPIRE   BANJO   SUGAR

THE MEMOIRS OF SHERLOCK HOLMES

21. Silver Blaze

'Is there any other point to which you would wish to draw my attention?'
'To the curious incident of the dog in the night-time.'
'The dog did nothing in the night-time.'
'That was the curious incident,' remarked Sherlock Holmes.

THE ADVENTURE of Silver Blaze took Holmes and me down to King's Pyland on Dartmoor, where the training stable of Colonel Ross is situated. Silver Blaze – the Colonel's champion five-year-old horse and first favourite for the Wessex Cup – had mysteriously disappeared during the night. As two of the Colonel's grooms searched for the missing horse early next morning, they found the trainer John Stalker lying dead on the moor about a quarter of a mile from the stables.

Inspector Gregory, to whom the case was committed, arrested one Fitzroy Simpson, who had been seen acting suspiciously around the stables that night. But Holmes suspected that there was more to the case than this, and that the police were holding the wrong man for the crime. He rambled about the room with his chin upon his chest and his brows knitted for a whole day; and at breakfast announced that he would have to go to Dartmoor in person.

I was glad to accompany him, and we set off from Paddington. As readers of my little accounts of Holmes's cases may recall, it was on this very journey that he astonished me by announcing suddenly that our rate of speed was 53 and one-half miles per hour. He explained: 'The telegraph posts upon this line are 60 yards apart, and the calculation is a simple one.'

It hardly seemed simple to me. I never got to work it out, because Holmes immediately pressed on to outline to me the details of this singular case.

But it was a long journey, and even at that speed we would not reach our destination until near nightfall, so our conversation turned to more general subjects. I cannot remember why – it might have been the association with fire in the name 'Silver Blaze' perhaps – but we found ourselves talking about various conflagrations, both tragic and festive, from the past.

'I remember the spectacular bonfire party which my old regiment threw to celebrate the Queen's Jubilee,' said I. 'Our old quartermaster, Higgins, arranged everything. The pyrotechnics were so astonishing that even to this day I still remember the precise number of all the different fireworks that he had arranged.'

And to show off to my friend that I could really do it, I recited the list. 'There were 210 rockets; 672 firecrackers, 168 squibs and 294 sparklers,' I recounted.

'How very singular,' said Holmes. 'And were you by chance treated to any potatoes, cooked in the fire?'

'Oh, yes,' said I. 'I scarcely recall the exact number, but . . .'

'But it was a superfluity of potatoes, was it not, Watson? Ha! That old quartermaster of yours must have had a fine sense of humour to bake so many potatoes for your little gathering!'

'But, Holmes, how could you know how many potatoes . . . ?'

'My dear fellow, is it not obvious? From the information you have already given me, I can calculate precisely how many potatoes Higgins prepared for the regiment. And so can you, Watson, if you reason it out.'

'Come, now,' he said, glancing at his watch. 'We have precisely twelve minutes before we alight at Tavistock. In that time, can you tell me how many potatoes there were?'

22. The Yellow Face

'Pipes are occasionally of extraordinary interest,' said he. 'Nothing has more individuality, save perhaps watches and bootlaces. The indications here, however, are neither very marked nor very important. The owner is obviously a muscular man, left-handed, with an excellent set of teeth, careless in his habits, and with no need to practise economy.'

'WATSON,' SAID Mr Sherlock Holmes to me after this case, 'if it should ever strike you that I am getting a little over-confident in my powers, or giving less pains to a case than it deserves, kindly whisper "Norbury" in my ear, and I shall be infinitely obliged to you.' For it was in Norbury that the happy home of Mr Grant Munro was suddenly disrupted by the very peculiar behaviour of his wife, Effie, and other strange occurrences locally.

Not only did Mrs Grant Munro ask for money without explanation; but she also stole out secretly at night. At the same time, a new tenant had moved into the nearby cottage, just the other side of the field; but on visiting, Mr Munro was rebuffed in churlish fashion by the housekeeper. And he was alarmed to see a face at one of the upper windows – a face of a livid chalky white, and with something set and rigid about it which was shockingly unnatural.

'I am afraid that this is a bad business, Watson,' said my friend after hearing Mr Munro's story. 'There's blackmail in it, or I am much mistaken.'

'You have a theory?'

'Yes, a provisional one. But I shall be surprised if it does not turn out to be correct. This woman's first husband is in that cottage.'

Well, in fact, Holmes's theory turned out to be some distance from the mark – hence the salutary effect of the "Norbury" mantra. But still, we could do nothing more until we had further news from our client, and so we sat down to our tea in Baker Street and started musing on other subjects.

'I have heard of Mr Munro's little village,' I said to my friend at last. 'It's apparently quite a picturesque spot.'

'Quite so,' replied Sherlock Holmes. 'Indeed, I once heard of a wealthy American visitor who liked the place so much that he offered $2 to each male and $4 to each female living there. All the males claimed the money, but only half of the females.'

'Nevertheless, that must have cost him quite a pretty penny,' I ventured.

46

'He gave away a total of $112,' replied Holmes, whose memory for such trivia could be quite formidable.

'So how many people lived in the village at that time?' I asked, quite innocently.

Holmes looked at me scornfully, as if to say that he had already given me that information. And with a little effort, I found that I could indeed work it out myself.

23. The Stock-broker's Clerk

'I perceive that you have been unwell lately. Summer colds are always a little trying.'

'I was confined to the house by a severe chill for three days last week. I thought, however, that I had cast off every trace of it.'

'So you have. You look remarkably robust.'

'How, then, did you know of it?'

'My dear fellow, you know my methods.'

'You deduced it, then?'

'Certainly.'

'And from what?'

'From your slippers.'

MR HALL Pycroft, a stock-broker's clerk who was looking for work, received a job offer which seemed to be too good to be true – as indeed, it turned out to be.

One Mr Arthur Pinner, whose card described him as a 'financial agent', told him that he had far too much ability for the position at Mawson & Williams's in Lombard Street which he was proposing to accept. 'By Monday,' he said, 'you will be the business manager of the Franco-Midland Hardware Company, Limited, with 134 branches in the towns and villages of France, not counting one in Brussels and one in San Remo.' The promised salary was handsome too, and even that would be more than doubled by commissions.

'Be in Birmingham tomorrow at one,' said Mr Pinner, directing Pycroft to the company's offices at 126B Corporation Street. But the offices turned out to be a couple of empty, dusty rooms at the top of a very lofty staircase. There, he was given a large directory of Paris merchants to work through.

He undertook this task with due diligence; though his suspicions about his new employers were strained to breaking point when he observed that the company's Birmingham agent – whom Mr Pinner said was his brother, Harry – had precisely the same sort of gold filling in precisely the same tooth as his London sibling.

Could they be one and the same person? If so, why should he go to these elaborate lengths to deceive a humble stock-broker's clerk?

'And then suddenly it struck me,' continued our client, 'that what was dark to me might be very light to Mr Sherlock Holmes.'

The case was soon commanding the whole concentration of my friend the detective. We hardly drew another word from him until we were in New Street. Nevertheless, he did break his silence once on the train journey, to set a little conundrum for myself and Mr Pycroft to solve. (In all honesty, I think he was finding our idle chat somewhat distracting to his introspections about the case, and he surmised, correctly, that the problem would occupy us more quietly for a while.) Anyway, here is how it ran.

'Stock-brokers are supposed to be good with figures, Mr Pycroft, so consider this' – Holmes scrawled the following set of numbers on a sheet of paper:

4	3	2	6	8	9
1	5	7	2	7	7
2	4	3	1	?	?

'Now, which numbers should replace the question marks?' And he folded his arms, drew even more deeply on his pipe, and creased his brow in silent concentration once again.

24. The 'Gloria Scott'

'Come, now, Mr Holmes,' said he, laughing good-humouredly. 'I'm an excellent subject, if you can deduce anything from me.'

'I fear there is not very much,' I answered. 'I might suggest that you have gone about in fear of some personal attack within the last twelvemonth.'

The laugh faded from his lips, and he stared at me in great surprise . . .

'Anything else?' he asked, smiling.

'You have boxed a good deal in your youth.'

'Right again . . . .Anything else?'
'You have done a good deal of digging by your callosities.'
'Made all my money at the gold fields.'
'You have been in New Zealand.'
'Right again.'
'You have visited Japan.'
'Quite true.'
'And you have been most intimately associated with someone whose initials were J.A., and whom you afterwards were eager to entirely forget.'
Mr Trevor stood slowly up, fixed his large blue eyes upon me with a strange wild stare, and then pitched forward . . . in a dead faint.

THE CASE of the *Gloria Scott* is of special interest because it was the very first in which Sherlock Holmes was ever engaged as a detective. Mr Victor Trevor – the only friend which the introspective Holmes ever made during his two years at college – had invited him down to his father's place at Donnithorpe, in Norfolk, for a month of the long vacation.

But the peace of the Trevor family was shattered by the arrival, one day, of a seaman with a cringing manner and shambling gait. His appearance seemed to unsettle Trevor's father. And within a few weeks the sinister fellow had achieved a strange mastery over the household. He had been appointed gardener, then promoted to butler. The maids complained about his vile language and drunken habits; but instead of dismissing him, Trevor Senior simply raised the wages of the other servants by way of redress. At last, the man would threaten and insult family members themselves, without any rebuke being issued by the father.

A little later, Trevor's father received an enigmatic note about pheasants and other game, which so convulsed him with terror that he suffered a stroke and passed into an unconsciousness from which he never recovered.

The note turned out to be a coded message; and its decryption allowed Holmes to solve the mystery and explain these strange events.

As I was looking over that very paper, which Holmes had kept as a memento of his first case, I could not help noticing some other coded messages which he had preserved alongside – some stray notes, possibly, for his intended short monograph on codes and code-breaking. One of these ran as follows:

F 29 W

A 10 I

I 29 T

R 21 C

Y ?? H

'What could be the connection between FAIRY and WITCH and the numbers?' I asked myself. 'And what number should replace the question marks?'

25. The Musgrave Ritual

'You know my methods in such cases, Watson. I put myself in the man's place, and, having first gauged his intelligence, I try

*to imagine how I should myself have proceeded under the same
circumstances. In this case the matter was simplified by
Brunton's intelligence being quite first-rate, so that it was
unnecessary to make any allowance for the personal
equation . . .'*

SHERLOCK HOLMES had not seen Reginald Musgrave in
four years, since the time they were at college together.

Now Musgrave was master of the Manor House at
Hurleston in western Sussex (perhaps the oldest inhabited
building in the county); and he walked into Holmes's room
in Montague Street, near the British Museum, to report a
strange combination of events that had troubled his
household.

Brunton, the butler, had been found in the library,
furtively studying some of the private family documents
which he had removed from the bureau.

The particular paper which occupied this clandestine
study recorded a queer set of questions and answers that
made up the Musgrave Ritual, that strange and seemingly
pointless catechism which all the Musgraves were required
to know by heart upon reaching manhood. Although it
seemed of no importance in itself, Musgrave was shocked
at the man's breach of trust, and gave him a week to quit
the premises.

On the third morning, however, in came the maid,
Rachel Howells, screaming and sobbing; while Brunton had
disappeared. All his property was in his room, apart from
his suit and slippers, but the butler himself was nowhere to
be found. Then, two days later, the maid disappeared too.
A drag of the lake, where her footsteps seemed to lead,
brought up only a linen bag full of metal and glass.

Holmes decided to go down to Sussex with Musgrave by
the first train. Although his travelling companion had a

52

quiet and diffident manner, Holmes never welcomed distractions at this stage of a case, when his mind was racing over facts and theories. So he set Musgrave a little problem to keep him occupied through the journey.

'Tell me, Musgrave,' he said. 'What is the connection between the words SEASHELL, HELMET, CLOAKROOM and BONFIRE?'

'Why, Mr Holmes, I'm sure I have no clue,' replied the latter.

'Then bring your memory to reflect on the grounds of Hurleston Manor, and your strange ritual. Then you should soon come up with the answer. In the meantime, please grant me the favour of a few minutes of silence!'

26. The Reigate Squire

'And now I made a very careful examination of the corner of paper which the inspector had submitted to us. It was at once clear to me that it formed part of a very remarkable document. Here it is. Do you not now observe something very suggestive about it?'
'It has a very irregular look,' said the Colonel.
'My dear sir,' cried Holmes, 'there cannot be the least doubt in the world that it has been written by two persons doing alternate words.'

IN THE April of '87, a telegram alerted me to the poor state of health of Mr Sherlock Holmes. I found him exhausted from having completed (successfully) an investigation that had extended over two months, during which he had never worked less than fifteen hours a day and had more than once, as he assured me, kept to his task for more than five days at a stretch.

I prescribed complete rest and a change of air, and prevailed on my old Army friend, Colonel Hayter, to put us up for a week at his country house near Reigate in Surrey.

However, Holmes's sleuth-hound senses soon started twitching at the news that the home of one of the local magnates had been burgled – though only a book, two candlesticks, a letter-weight, a barometer and a ball of twine had been taken.

When, next morning, we learned that the coachman at another nearby house had been found shot dead, it had become clear that our week in the country would *not* be the relaxed rest-cure in the springtime countryside that I had intended.

By a most thorough investigation of the scene of the murder, Holmes was able to unravel the twisted thread of greed, blackmail and deception which had led to it. I must confess that he returned to Baker Street much refreshed and invigorated by the diversion.

On our first evening at Colonel Hayter's, when I abjured my friend not to get involved in the burglary matter, I thought for a while that I had succeeded in forcing him to take a complete rest. As I held up a warning finger, he shrugged his shoulders with a glance of comic resignation towards the Colonel, and the talk drifted away into less dangerous channels.

'Fine library you have here, Colonel,' said my friend and patient.

'It's one of my consuming hobbies,' replied our host. 'These finely bound volumes of Dickens's works give me particular pleasure.'

'Then did you know,' continued Holmes without a

pause, before the Colonel could even reach down one of his treasured collection, 'that in a single year, the publisher of those very works claimed to have sold 1,657 copies of DAVID COPPERFIELD, 1,251 copies of A CHRISTMAS CAROL and 202 copies of THE PICKWICK PAPERS?'

'My dear Mr Holmes! Your knowledge astonishes me.'

'It's nothing, Colonel, the figures are trivial to remember because of their quite singular nature. Dr Watson can probably tell you how many copies of NICHOLAS NICKLEBY were sold. We will give him ten minutes; that should be enough for such a problem! And then I am sure that my doctor will insist that I retire to bed.'

27. The Crooked Man

'I have the advantage of knowing your habits, my dear Watson,' said he. 'When your round is a short one you walk, and when it is a long one you use a hansom. As I perceive that your boots, although used, are by no means dirty, I cannot doubt that you are at present busy enough to justify the hansom.'

'Excellent!' I cried.

'Elementary,' said he. 'It is one of those instances where the reasoner can produce an effect which seems remarkable to his neighbour, because the latter has missed the one little point which is the basis of the deduction.'

LATE ONE summer evening, just a few months after my marriage, Holmes burst in on me to ask that I should join him on an investigation in Aldershot the next day.

Colonel James Barclay, of the Royal Munsters (one of the most famous Irish regiments in the British Army), had been found dead in a pool of blood at his villa near the camp. The coachman, alerted by a loud crash and a piercing scream from the morning-room, but unable to break down the door, went outside and broke in through a window. He found Barclay dead near the hearth; and the Colonel's wife, Nancy, in a state of insensibility upon a couch. The door of the room was locked, but no key could be found either in the room or upon the person of Mrs Barclay.

There had been other unusual occurrences. The servants had heard a violent argument going on immediately before the tragedy. In the quarrel, they had heard Mrs Barclay refer to 'David', though of course the Colonel's name was James. Miss Morrison, a young lady from the next villa, had accompanied Mrs Barclay to a meeting of the Guild of St George earlier that evening; and although on their return they met a strange, crooked man in the street, she could give no reason why her companion had arrived home in such evident ill-humour.

The case proved to be a story of betrayal, shame, and tragic accident. Holmes quickly and sure-footedly pursued his quarry like an accomplished hunter, and the full explanation soon came out.

To get to Aldershot, we took the 11.10 train from Waterloo. And before Holmes fell into that intense silence that always came over him as he was contemplating a case, I tried to engage him in some idle gossip about what had happened to each of us since I left Baker Street for my own hearth. But he was unwilling to be distracted, and stymied my gossip by setting me one of those annoying little puzzles of his.

'Look over there, Watson! On the road alongside the rail-track: a fire-engine on its way to some conflagration!'

'Why yes,' I replied, 'though its water-tank seems to be leaking. I do hope it will arrive in time!'

'Quite so, Watson. Now let us presume that the fire is at some house in the next settlement, which I estimate' – he took out his pocket-watch and glanced briefly at the roadway – 'is four and one-quarter miles away, and that the engine will continue at its present speed, which I calculate to be precisely fourteen and one-half miles per hour.'

I was used to my friend's instantaneous computations of speed and distance. 'It would arrive in just a few minutes,' I observed.

'Watson! You scintillate today. Now, if the tank of this same fire-engine presently contains 150 gallons of water; if it leaks 10 gallons per hour while on the move; and if, furthermore, it requires 147 gallons of water to put out the fire; then tell me, my dear Watson, do you think it will succeed in its mission?'

Holmes's ruse to distract me worked wonderfully, for in a moment I found myself deep in thought as I calculated the answer.

28. The Resident Patient

It was ten o'clock before we reached Baker Street again. A brougham was waiting at our door.
'Hum! A doctor's – general practitioner, I perceive,' said Holmes. 'Not long in practice, but has a good deal to do. Come to consult us, I fancy! Lucky we came back!'

I REMEMBER the following puzzle very well, for Holmes put it to me on a rainy October evening that will remain lodged in my mind for a good long time – the same evening on which we found Dr Percy Trevelyan's brougham waiting at our door, and heard of the curious behaviour of his landlord and patient.

The latter was a gentleman of the name of Blessington, who came to Dr Trevelyan as a complete stranger, and yet offered to take a house in Brook Street, furnish it, pay the maids, and set him up in medical practice. Blessington himself, who had a weak heart and needed constant medical supervision, lived at the house in the character of a resident patient.

But Dr Trevelyan's life took an even odder turn when a Russian nobleman and his son were announced at his consulting-room one evening. The son waited outside as the consultation proceeded. But then the patient appeared to suffer a dreadful seizure from which he could not be roused. Dr Trevelyan ran down to his laboratory for nitrite of amyl, which he had found effective in such cases; but on returning he was surprised to find that both men had disappeared.

He was even more astonished when they returned the next day, explaining their rapid disappearance as a result of the older man's amnesia following his seizure. Again the son waited outside while Dr Trevelyan examined the father. But from that moment, Mr Blessington seemed to be in a state of high fear and agitation. What could be the explanation?

The case later turned to tragedy, but it was this sequence of strange events that brought the doctor's brougham to our door, where we found it as we returned from a three-hour ramble through London.

On our walk, Holmes's characteristic talk, with its keen

The Napoleaon of crime.

observance of detail and subtle power of inference, kept me enthralled the whole time.

One of those questions of inference I remember particularly well, because he set me to solve it, and because it had an appropriate medical connection.

'Let me give you a list of words, Watson! All you have to do is to change the first letter of each word to the left and to the right. Two other English words must be formed as a result.' And he drew out the list with his finger on the dusty window-pane of some unoccupied shop, so:

LARGE __ LEAST

PEACH __ PATIO

SCORN __ SPACE

CRATE __ CRONY

TASTY __ TAILS

'Place the replacement letter that you have used,' he continued, 'in the empty space in the middle. When you have completed this exercise for all the words I have listed, you will find that another word can be read downwards. What is it?'

I gazed hard at what he had written, and scratched my head as I contemplated the solution.

29. The Greek Interpreter

'Look at these two men who are coming towards us,
for example.'
'The billiard-marker and the other?'
'Precisely. What do you make of the other?'
. . . 'An old soldier, I perceive,' said Sherlock.
'And very recently discharged,' remarked the brother.
'Served in India, I see.'
'And a non-commissioned officer.'
'Royal Artillery, I fancy,' said Sherlock.
'And a widower.'
'But with a child.'
'Children, my dear boy, children.'

MYCROFT HOLMES might indeed have possessed powers of observation and deduction that were superior even to those of his younger brother – as the latter insisted was the case. But while these abilities made him a most valuable part of the machinery of Her Majesty's Government, his lack of ambition and energy left him quite unsuited to practical detective work, where physical action was often as essential as those mental qualities.

So it was fortunate that his younger sibling happened to visit him at the Diogenes Club at just the right time to help solve an unpleasant case involving his neighbour, Mr Melas, a Greek interpreter.

The latter was a short, stout man, whose olive face and coal-black hair proclaimed his Southern origin. He told us how he had been asked, that Monday night, to accompany a Mr Latimer to a Kensington address to help translate some business matters between himself and a Greek friend. But he was surprised that the windows of the carriage had been papered over to prevent him seeing the route that they took; and Latimer made it clear that the interpreter had no choice but to go along with him in this strange adventure.

At their final destination, Mr Melas was required to translate some very threatening questions delivered to a man who was obviously being held under restraint, and whose face was disguised to prevent recognition. He established the name of the captive as Paul Kratides, and discovered that there was a woman in the house whose first name was Sophy.

The interpreter's story started the three of us upon the investigation of a sensational case. Nevertheless, it was sheer good fortune that Holmes and I learnt about it only because a chance remark from the detective had made me curious enough to meet this previously unknown brother.

It was a fine summer evening, and after tea in Baker Street our conversation had roamed in a desultory, spasmodic fashion from golf clubs to the causes of the change in the obliquity of the ecliptic, and came round at last to the question of atavism and hereditary aptitudes, in which the name of Mr Mycroft Holmes was quite naturally mentioned.

During our discussion on astronomical subjects, Holmes threw out the following question:

'A planet completes an orbit of the sun in 4 years, and another completes one in 28 years. They are now in line with each other and the sun on the same side and follow clockwise orbits. When will the two planets next form a straight line with each other and the sun, eh, Watson?'

30. The Naval Treaty

'You are confident that the thief came in a cab?'
'If not, there is no harm done. But if Mr Phelps is correct
in saying that there is no hiding-place either in the room
or the corridors, then the person must have come from
outside. If he came from outside on so wet a night, and yet left
no trace of damp upon the linoleum, which was examined
within a few minutes of his passing, then it is exceedingly
probable that he came in a cab. Yes, I think that we may safely
deduce a cab.'

A N OLD school-fellow of mine, Percy Phelps, wrote to
prevail on me to see whether I could interest my
friend Mr Sherlock Holmes in a most unfortunate mystery
which had blighted his career in the Foreign Office. The
tone was so pitiable, that of course I rushed round to the
old rooms in Baker Street, where I found my friend, test-
tube in hand, confirming the criminality of some unfortunate wretch. 'A very commonplace little murder,' he
explained. 'You've got something better, I fancy.'

With that case now solved and behind him, I was able
to induce Holmes to go to Woking to get the facts of the
case from Phelps. The latter explained what had occurred.
It seems that he had been given the job of copying a long
document, an important naval treaty, in the French
language. He was engaged on the task at his Whitehall
office until late into the night, and so ordered a cup of
coffee to clear his brain.

When, some time later, the coffee had still not come,
he went down to the lodge by the main door, where he
found the kettle boiling furiously, but the commissionaire

asleep. Just as he was about to wake the man, the job was done for him by a loud bell – indeed, the bell of the room in which he had just been working. Horrified that someone should be in the room where the precious naval treaty lay unattended, he rushed back, to find the room empty and the original document stolen.

After hearing the whole story, Holmes and I were soon whirling back up to London in a Portsmouth train. Holmes was sunk in profound thought and hardly opened his mouth until we had passed Clapham Junction. It was twenty past three when we reached our terminus, and we made time only for a hasty luncheon at the buffet before we pushed on at once to Scotland Yard.

Over luncheon, Holmes amused me with the following, rather annoying rhyme:

'Its first is in BUTTER but not in BREAD
'Its next is in HAIR but not in HEAD
'Its third is in BIKE and also in RIDE
'Its fourth is in ICE but not in SLIDE
'Its last is in WHISKER and also in KITTEN
'The whole may be done by a magician
'What is it?'

31. The Final Problem

'He is the Napoleon of crime, Watson. He is the organizer of half that is evil and of nearly all that is undetected in this great city.'

O N THE EVENING of 24th April 1891, Sherlock Holmes walked into my consulting-room in a state of some agitation. The cause for his concern was that he was being pursued by agents of Professor Moriarty, the brilliant mathematician who Holmes told me was responsible for half the crime in London, and whose arrest would clear up forty mysteries.

But Moriarty was not a man to fall silently into the net woven by Sherlock Holmes, and had pledged the destruction of The Great Detective. So Holmes decided that it would be better to absent himself for a few days until the police were in a position to close the net and put him out of danger.

Thus we found ourselves slipping out of Victoria station on the boat train, just in time to avoid the Professor himself. We had to throw him off our trail again at Canterbury. From there we went to Newhaven, then over to Brussels, then Strasbourg, on our way towards Geneva.

It was a trip which was to end in a much-reported episode of violence and tragedy at the Reichenbach Falls.

But before then, for a charming week, we wandered up the valley of the Rhône, and then, by way of Interlaken, to Meiringen. As we strolled over the mountains, admiring the dainty green of the spring below, and the virgin white of the winter above, we of course had plenty of time to discuss some of our more extraordinary cases, such as that of Vanberry, the wine merchant, or Colonel Warburton's madness, and our encounters with Ricoletti of the club foot and his abominable wife. We had time, moreover, for a good deal of idle banter; though never for one instant did I imagine that Holmes had forgotten the shadow which lay across him.

Even the little intellectual diversions he set for me

betrayed the fact that he still had Professor Moriarty in mind.

'Here's a *mathematical* puzzle for you, Watson!' he said one day, as we stopped to take in the majestic scenery of the spot. 'Which number should replace the question mark?' And with a stick he scratched into the earth the following pattern.

6	9	6	7	5
1	1	8	1	9
4	8	?	5	7

THE HOUND OF THE BASKERVILLES

32. The Curse of the Baskervilles

'In my experience it is only an amiable man in this world who receives testimonials, only an unambitious one who abandons a London career for the country, and only an absent-minded one who leaves his stick and not a visiting card after waiting an hour in your room.'
'And the dog?'
'Has been in the habit of carrying this stick behind his master. Being a heavy stick the dog has held it tightly by the middle, and the marks of his teeth are clearly visible. The dog's jaw, as shown in the space between these marks, is too broad in my opinion for a terrier and not broad enough for a mastiff. It may have been – yes, by Jove, it is a curly-haired spaniel.'

I HAVE always regarded *The Hound of the Baskervilles* as Sherlock Holmes's most perfect case. There were cases he resolved more cleverly or more quickly, but none in which he played so active a part. Without his intervention a crime of monstrous proportion would have been success-fully committed. He saved the life and property of his client, and helped rid the world of a vicious and evil criminal mind.

The case began innocuously enough, with the arrival in our rooms of Dr James Mortimer. Holmes had already deduced much about him from the walking stick he had left, but nothing prepared us for his story. He read from a 1742 manuscript how the wicked Sir Hugo Baskerville had set the dogs on a maiden who resisted his fancy. Sir Hugo had been killed by a gigantic hound, whose curse was said to lie upon the family ever since.

Dr Mortimer then read us a news report of the recent death of Sir Charles Baskerville. He had been found dead, with strangely distorted face, one evening in the famous yew alley of Baskerville Hall, which lay deep in the moors of Dorsetshire. Dr Mortimer told us something which was not in the report, namely that he had seen the footprints of a gigantic hound near the body. He asked us to help when the new heir, Sir Henry Baskerville, arrived from Canada.

While we were waiting after breakfast for Dr Mortimer and Sir Henry to appear at ten, Holmes ringed some letters in *The Times* and passed it across to me. He had put the letters in four groups:

S C   D E   N T   B U
H R   I S   P O   T L

'Here, Watson. Select two letters from each group of four. If you have chosen the correct letters you will then be able to rearrange them to spell something best eaten hot.'

He glanced at the pocket-watch on the mantelpiece. 'We have a full ten minutes before our guests arrive,' he observed. 'That should be time enough to do it!' And he picked up another newspaper from the day's pile.

He paid almost no attention to me as I struggled with the letters, preferring instead to scour the agony columns from which so much information of professional import-ance could be gleaned by a consulting detective.

When, ten minutes later, I was no nearer to the answer, and the sound of two footfalls on the stairs heralded the punctual arrival of Dr Mortimer and Sir Henry, he said only, 'Tut, tut.'

33. Sir Henry Baskerville

My first impression as I opened the door was that a fire had broken out, for the room was so filled with smoke that the light of the lamp upon the table was blurred by it. As I entered, however, my fears were set at rest, for it was the acrid fumes of strong, coarse tobacco which took me by the throat and set me coughing. Through the haze I had a vague vision of Holmes in his dressing-gown coiled up in an armchair with his black clay pipe between his lips. Several rolls of paper lay around him.

'Caught cold, Watson?' said he.

WHEN DR MORTIMER brought Sir Henry to Baker Street next day, the latter had received an anony-mous letter at his lodging in the Northumberland Hotel – just next to the Turkish bath which Holmes and I occasionally frequented – warning him away from the moor. He had also, quite mysteriously, lost a new boot.

As they left, Holmes took me to trail them at some distance, and only just failed to grab whoever was tailing them from a hansom cab. Since there was obviously some villainy afoot, my esteemed friend sent me back to the moor with Sir Henry, while some pressing business detained him in London. I was given strict instructions to report regularly.

Honoured as I was to be so trusted by Holmes, I was somewhat apprehensive when he told Sir Henry not to go out alone, and advised me to keep my revolver near me day and night.

We were all intrigued to learn that Sir Henry had found his new boot, but had now lost an old one.

Holmes had told me to keep a special eye on everyone who would come into contact with Sir Henry at Baskerville Hall. From the Hall itself there were the Barrymore couple who acted as servants, and a groom. There were two moorland farmers, and Dr Mortimer and his wife. Also nearby was a naturalist called Stapleton, with his sister, and a Mr Frankland of Lafter Hall.

I confirmed that I would be careful, and said I would treat everyone in the vicinity as a prime suspect.

'Interesting word, *prime*.' He smiled. 'In mathematics, as you know, it refers to any number divisible only by itself and one.'

I vaguely recalled hearing the same thing from a rather dull schoolteacher more years ago than I cared to admit.

'You can,' Holmes continued without pause, 'make a series of nine-digit numbers by putting all of the digits from 1 through 9 in any order.'

'Indeed,' I replied, 'and a great many of them at that.'

'Yes, there are of course precisely – but I digress. Tell

me only: How many of those numbers are prime?' asked Holmes, taking hold of my pocket-watch and flicking it open.

'Good heavens, Holmes! I have no idea,' I expostulated.

'On the contrary, Watson, you can tell me in less than three minutes,' he challenged.

I have to admit I could not.

34. Baskerville Hall

'There is as much difference to my eyes between the leaded bourgeois type of a Times *article and the slovenly print of an evening half-penny paper as there could be between your negro and your Esquimeau. The detection of types is one of the most elementary branches of knowledge to the special expert in crime, though I confess that once when I was very young I confused the* Leeds Mercury *with the* Western Morning News. *But a* Times *leader is entirely distinctive, and these words could have been taken from nothing else.'*

AS WE MADE our way to the Hall by carriage after our train ride to Devonshire, the driver explained that the soldiers we kept seeing were looking out for the escaped convict, Selden, the Notting Hill murderer. The thought of that fiend out on the moor made it seem even more dark and forbidding than it already was. Then we saw Baskerville Hall, glimmering like a ghost at the end of its long drive.

Sir Henry and I both found the place very gloomy, and retired early following a subdued meal. During the night I fancied I heard a woman sob somewhere in that great dark place, a fact which Sir Henry confirmed next day. My foreboding was reinforced when I met the Stapletons later; as I was talking to the naturalist we both heard a long, low, sad moan echo across the moor from the vicinity of the Grimpen Mire. Stapleton's sister gave me a terse warning to head straight back to London.

However, I had to perform the duties which my friend had entrusted to me. When I sent my first full report to Holmes – it was then October the 13th – I was able to tell him that Sir Henry had taken a real fancy to Beryl Stapleton. I also reported on Mr Frankland of Lafter Hall, a litigious man who seemed to make a hobby of frivolous lawsuits.

The most exciting news I gave Holmes, however, was that I had seen the servant Barrymore signalling from the Hall at night by waving a candle at a window. I knew not who received his message, but I did know it was a betrayal of trust of his new master, and showed great ingratitude after Sir Henry had given the man a considerable part of his old wardrobe.

My second report, on October the 15th, told of two exciting incidents. Despite all of my friend's warnings, Sir Henry went out on the moor alone to meet Miss Stapleton. Against my better judgement I let him go, but, repenting instantly, I followed him and arrived in time to see Stapleton himself come across the couple, and go berserk with rage.

Not only this, but I was proud to tell Holmes that, with Sir Henry's help, I solved the mystery of the candle signals. The two of us pounced on Barrymore as he signalled again that night, and forced him to explain. The fiend Selden, living as an outcast on the moor, turned out to be Eliza Barrymore's brother. The Barrymores had been leaving him

The Hound of the Baskervilles

food and signalling its location with a candle at the window.

Sir Henry and I hurried out, I with my old service

revolver, to apprehend the escaped murderer. Alas, the miscreant eluded our pursuit, but we both heard again the dreadful wailing of a hound, from the direction of the great Grimpen Mire. Not only that, but I also saw the silhouette of a tall, thin man outlined against the silver moon. I am afraid the conundrum seemed to be growing more complicated rather than less.

I then discovered from Barrymore that Sir Charles had received a note on the night of his death, and that although burned, it still showed the initials L. L. on the charred fragments. Dr Mortimer told us this could be Laura Lyons, the daughter of Frankland, the amateur lawyer.

When I confronted the woman I soon overcame her pitiful denial. She had written the letter, and had arranged to meet Sir Charles on the night of his strange death, but she had not kept the assignation. I was contemplating this new fact when I met Frankland himself on my way home. A tip from him enabled me to track down the mysterious stranger whose outline I had seen while chasing the convict.

Imagine my surprise when my search led to a small stone hut on the moor, and I found that the stranger was none other than Holmes himself! He had been hiding on the moor to make his own observations. I was most put out that Holmes had not trusted me, but he reassured me that my work had been invaluable, and showed all of my reports which had been sent on to him.

He also confirmed that there was a *real* hound. 'Now, Watson,' he warned, 'you must be as alert as ever you were in the Afghan WARS. We shall hear this hound PANT, we shall know it by its EARS, and we shall expose it at LAST.'

'Rather florid way of putting it, Holmes.'

'Just idle amusement, Watson. If you take those four

words – WARS, PANT, EARS and LAST – and insert the same two letters in the middle of each of them, you will find they form four new English words.'

By the end of the five minutes he had allotted me to solve this riddle, I had regained a little of my self-esteem, but was no nearer to the answer.

35. Death on the Moor

At the same instant Lestrade gave a yell of terror and threw himself face downward upon the ground. I sprang to my feet, my inert hand grasping my pistol, my mind paralyzed by the dreadful shape which had sprung out upon us from the shadows of the fog. A hound it was, an enormous coal-black hound, but not such a hound as mortal eyes have ever seen. Fire burst from its open mouth, its eyes glowed with a smouldering glare, its muzzle and hackles and dewlap were outlined in flickering flame. Never in the delirious dream of a disordered brain could anything more savage, more appalling, more hellish be conceived than that dark form and savage face which broke upon us out of the wall of fog.

HOLMES WAS just explaining to me that he had deduced murder, 'refined, cold-blooded, deliberate murder', when we heard a dreadful anguished scream. We ran, but arrived too late. We saw the dead body and recognized Sir Henry's jacket. Holmes was beside himself with remorse until we realized that the body was that of Selden, the escaped convict, wearing Sir Henry's jacket.

My most excellent friend and companion told me he

had been saved by sheer luck from allowing his client to die. Now he resolved to set his trap with due celerity. We found that Sir Henry had been invited on to the moor by Stapleton, but had heeded our warnings and stayed in. Meanwhile, the Barrymores had given some of Sir Henry's old clothes to the convict, and the wretch had been killed in place of the baronet.

To my astonishment Holmes then told Sir Henry to accept Stapleton's dinner invitation, and to walk home by night across the moor. It was a direct reversal of his previous dire warnings. Added to that, Holmes and I were to depart by train in the morning, leaving Sir Henry alone to his fate.

It was a stratagem. Holmes and I left the train at its first stop, picked up Inspector Lestrade from the London express, and travelled back to the moor at speed. We reached Stapleton's house and saw him dining with Sir Henry. To the great concern and distress of my companion, one of those devilish Dartmoor fogs descended upon us just as it was time for Sir Henry to begin his walk back. We heard his footsteps, followed by a continuous patter from within the fog.

As a gigantic hound attacked Sir Henry, Holmes and I fired together. It took several shots to kill the beast, but we were in time to save Sir Henry from the dreadful death which Stapleton had planned for him. We found Beryl Stapleton tied up in their cottage, but Stapleton had fled into the Grimpen Mire, which swallowed him to what I regarded as a well-deserved death.

Holmes pieced together the story for us. Stapleton was a Baskerville himself, and the next heir after Sir Henry. Beryl Stapleton was his wife, not his sister. He had used her as bait to ensnare Sir Henry, just as he had used Laura Lyons to lure Sir Charles to his death.

The hound was the most strong and savage dog that Stapleton could buy, and was treated with a new phosphorus preparation to make it more demonic. Holmes had guessed right from the start that there was a real hound, on account of the missing boots. He had not hesitated to expose himself to mortal danger to protect his client and bring to justice the most evil, the most dangerous adversary that we ever encountered.

In my opinion it was, as I say, Holmes's most perfect case. I was enormously proud that my illustrious friend had deployed so excellently the intellectual skills for which I made him famous. As for me, I was more than a little proud to have played what Holmes described as a pivotal role. Fated often to be the passive observer of my friend's genius, I was here privileged to protect, to observe, and at the end to be at my friend's side when it turned finally to dangerous action.

'It was,' he reflected, as we sat either side of a blazing fire in our sitting-room in Baker Street one evening towards the end of November, 'a case which turned back on itself. It began with the certainty of a hound and with evil from the mire. It ended with the extinction of the hound and with the mire swallowing its evil.'

'It's a good job you were there to turn things around,' I ventured.

'Well, it is not the only thing I have been turning round recently. For amusement I have been turning a few numbers back on themselves. I now know all of the numbers which, if their digits are reversed, give squares which are themselves the reverse of the squares of the original numbers. Excluding palindromes of course. I have found it to be a most singular and whimsical problem.'

When I professed not to understand, he made it clear.

'Take a number and square it. Now reverse the digits of

the original number and square that. I want all those where the square of the first is the reverse of the square of the second. Original numbers like 202, which read the same as their reverses, are not allowed.'

While I now understood the question, it was no easy task setting about the answer, even given the six minutes he described as 'more than adequate'. I produced a couple within the time, but one was a palindrome (the same in reverse). He showed me that there were at least two others in addition to my single valid answer.

THE RETURN OF SHERLOCK HOLMES

36. The Empty House

'You can trust us to look after that, Mr Holmes,' said
Lestrade, as the whole party moved towards the door.
'Anything further to say?'
'Only to ask what charge you intend to prefer?'
'What charge, sir? Why, of course, the attempted murder of
Mr Sherlock Holmes.'
'Not so, Lestrade. I do not propose to appear in the matter
at all. To you, and to you only, belongs the credit of the
remarkable arrest which you have effected. Yes, Lestrade, I
congratulate you! With your usual happy mixture of cunning
and audacity, you have got him.'
'Got him! Got whom, Mr Holmes?'
'The man that the whole force has been seeking in vain –
Colonel Sebastian Moran, who shot the Honourable Ronald
Adair with an expanding bullet from an air-gun through the
open window of the second-floor front of Number 427 Park
Lane, upon the thirtieth of last month. That's the charge,
Lestrade.'

I T WAS IN the spring of 1894 that all of London was interested, and the fashionable world dismayed, by the murder of the Honourable Ronald Adair under most unusual and inexplicable circumstances. He had arrived home from his club at exactly ten. But his mother, returning at eleven-twenty, could get no reply when she stopped by his room to wish him good-night. After much knocking and shouting to him, the locked door was forced. The unfortunate young man was found lying near the table. His head had taken a revolver bullet, though no weapon could be found.

This crime also aroused the professional interest of Mr Sherlock Holmes, whom I had not seen since that fateful day at the Reichenbach Falls, some three years earlier, and had presumed dead. Through my shock, he told me the remarkable story of what took place there; and promised me a notable new adventure for that very evening.

This was *The Adventure of the Empty House*. The building in question was exactly opposite our old lodging in Baker Street, where I was astonished to see in the window a perfectly convincing duplicate of my friend the detective. Our mission would capture the author of many vile crimes, including the apparently inexplicable death of Ronald Adair.

Anyway, we had a few minutes to while away before half-past nine, when (said my friend) our excursion would begin; but since we could hardly discuss the missing three years of our past in so short a time, he indicated his preference to leave that to a more suitable time, and instead cleared and occupied both our minds with a problem of less momentous proportions.

'I detect the hand of an expert marksman here, Watson,' he confided, 'and I am certain that I know who it is. There are few in England who could match his skill. I saw him once at a public exhibition of sharpshooting. From a distance of 50 yards, he achieved some truly remarkable scores, shooting targets no bigger than a penny.'

'I wonder that he hit any at all!'

'Well, the maximum possible score, for a bull's-eye on that minuscule target, was 25 points; the outer rings scored less. Our suspect did take a few shots to get his aim, scoring an average of 15 points on the first 30. Remarkable enough; but after another 10 shots, his average rose to 17 points.'

'He must have done exceedingly well on those last shots,' I ventured, 'considering the great distance.'

'Very true,' answered my friend, 'and if you ponder the matter you will be able to tell me: What was the average number of points he scored with the last 10 shots only? I think ten minutes should suffice for that little problem, Watson.'

37. The Norwood Builder

'You mentioned your name, as if I should recognize it, but I assure you that, beyond the obvious facts that you are a bachelor, a solicitor, a Freemason, and an asthmatic, I know nothing whatever about you.'

SOME MONTHS after Holmes's return, we had just finished breakfast one morning – my dear wife had died some time earlier and on Holmes's suggestion I had sold my practice and come back to share the old quarters in Baker Street – when our peace was disturbed by the most frantic ringing and beating on the door.

The pale and dishevelled young lawyer who burst in on us was the unhappy John Hector McFarlane, announcing that he expected soon to be arrested, unjustly, upon the charge of murdering Mr Jonas Oldacre, of Lower Norwood.

Mr Oldacre had consulted McFarlane professionally to prepare a will – one which, to his astonishment, named him as the principal beneficiary of all the Norwood builder's property. Having gone to Oldacre's house to sort through some legal documents and then retired to bed in a nearby hotel, McFarlane was astonished to read the newspaper reports of the following morning: that there were signs of a violent struggle at the house, that Oldacre had disappeared, that the builder's timber-store had been set ablaze, and that a warrant had been issued for his own arrest.

Indeed it had; and a few minutes later Inspector Lestrade arrived at Baker Street to take his man into custody.

As a result of his customary precision in observation and deduction, Holmes managed to solve the case, and clear McFarlane's name. But his investigation began not at the scene of the crime, but, to my surprise, at the home of McFarlane's parents.

'No, my dear fellow, I don't think you can help me,' said my friend when I proposed to accompany him. 'There is no prospect of danger, or I should not dream of stirring out without you. I trust that when I see you in the evening, I will be able to report that I have done something for this unfortunate youngster.' And off he went.

But, perhaps sensing my disappointment and knowing that my mind would be on the case until his late return, he paused just long enough to scribble a few notes on a page in his pocket-book, which he tore off and tossed over to me. As the door closed behind him I saw that he had left me one of his little puzzles, perhaps hoping that it would occupy me contentedly for a few minutes at least.

Watson [he had written] – this puzzle seems appropriate, given that the missing man is a housebuilder. Start at the letter G on the diagram below, move to adjacent letters and collect four letters each time. How many different ways are there of collecting the letters of the word GOLD?

[signed] Sherlock Holmes

PS: Watson, you may *not* move diagonally!

Underneath this was the drawing, made out like a caricature of a house, thus:

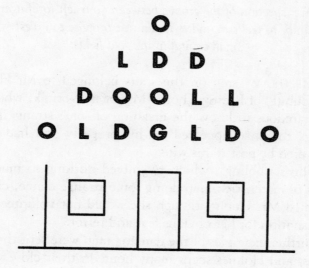

38. The Dancing Men

'You see, my dear Watson' – he propped his test-tube in the rack, and began to lecture with the air of a professor addressing his class -- 'it is not really difficult to construct a series of inferences, each dependent upon its predecessor and each simple in itself. If, after doing so, one simply knocks out all the central inferences and presents one's audience with the starting-point and the conclusion, one may produce a startling, though possibly a meretricious, effect. Now, it was not really difficult, by an inspection of the groove between your left forefinger and thumb, to feel sure that you did not propose to invest your small capital in the gold fields.'

THE HEAVY step on the stairs belonged to Mr Hilton Cubitt, of Riding Thorpe Manor in Norfolk, who was very anxious to know the meaning of some strange scribblings that had appeared on his property and had been delivered by post to his wife.

The scribblings, which resembled nothing so much as lines of matchstick-men doing some strange dance, clearly alarmed Mrs Cubitt; though she would not volunteer any explanation for her obvious fear and terror.

Further examples of the dancing men were sent through to us, and Holmes spent many hours in their close study. The next and tragic turn in the case was the discovery of the dead body of Mr Hilton Cubitt and his near-dead wife – both shot.

Mr Cubitt knew little of his American wife's past, and had met her only a year before, when up in London for the Jubilee. But Holmes reasoned that the dancing men were in reality examples of messages written in a code that she must have known. By decrypting the messages, Holmes was able to apprehend the individual who had unleashed this tragedy upon the household.

To Holmes, nevertheless, it was just another problem to be solved. 'Three-forty is our train,' he suddenly announced at the end of it, 'and I fancy we should be back in Baker Street for dinner.'

On the train home, my friend told me of some of the other methods he knew of for encrypting messages. One of these has stuck in my mind since that day. It read as follows:

```
N  M  O  T  C  E  P  O
T  O  A  I  T  U  T  E
D  R  V  A  O  S  S  R
-  Y  R  D  B  A  N  O
```

'What do you make of that, Watson? Amusing, no?' said my friend, handing over the scribbled paper and retiring back behind his evening newspaper.

At first I thought it was a completely indecipherable code, until I realized that, moving from letter to adjacent letter – vertically, horizontally or diagonally – one could spell out a short aphorism that I had recently noted in *Punch* magazine.

'I have it, Holmes!' I cried at last.

'Have what, Watson?'

'Why, the answer to your cryptogram,' I replied.

'Cryptogram? Oh, yes! My dear Watson, I gave you that so long ago that I had quite forgotten it by now! Surely it could not really have taken you so long?'

Sheepishly, I made some excuse and changed the subject of our conversation.

39. The Solitary Cyclist

'I nearly fell into the error of supposing that you were typewriting. Of course, it is obvious that it is music. You observe the spatulate finger-ends, Watson, which is common to both professions? There is a spirituality about the face, however' – she gently turned it towards the light – *'which the typewriter does not generate. This lady is a musician.'*
'Yes, Mr Holmes, I teach music.'
'In the country, I presume, from your complexion.'
'Yes, sir, near Farnham, on the borders of Surrey.'

IT WAS UPON Saturday, the 23rd of April in the year 1895 that we first heard of Miss Violet Smith, the Surrey music-teacher.

Four months before coming to us, she and her mother had seen in *The Times* an advertisement, enquiring of their whereabouts. Upon answering it, they met two gentlemen on a visit home from South Africa, a Mr Carruthers and a Mr Woodley. This pair reported that her uncle, Ralph Smith (who had gone to Africa twenty-five years before and not been heard of since) had died recently in Johannesburg, but had enjoined them to hunt up his relations, and see that they were in no want.

Mr Carruthers hired Miss Smith at a handsome salary as a music teacher for his daughter at Chiltern Grange near Farnham; and at first, this arrangement worked well. But then her happiness was shattered by the arrival of Mr Woodley, who made odious love to her, boasted of his wealth, and seized her in his arms in an attempt to extract a kiss. Carruthers threw him out, and she saw him no more.

But then, every week as she rode her bicycle to Farnham station on her way to visit her mother in town, she had been followed by a bearded man, also on a bicycle, riding about 200 yards behind. She tried, by varying her pace or by lying in wait at a corner, to shake him off and to establish his identity, but always failed.

Our client was distressed to the point of leaving Mr Carruthers's employment when the odious Mr Woodley reappeared – though now bearing some disfigurement, as if he had met with some accident. What could be the explanation of these odd events?

After a rather unsuccessful visit to Sussex by me, Holmes determined that we should both go down. It was a glorious morning, and the two of us walked along the broad, sandy road inhaling the morning air and rejoicing in the music of the birds and the fresh breath of the spring.

'Watson,' remarked my friend at this point. 'Suppose Miss Smith pedals up the hill at 5 miles per hour and races down, over the same distance, at 20 miles per hour. What do you suppose would be her average speed for the whole journey?'

'Why, Holmes, I haven't the faintest idea,' I replied, 'but I am sure I can work it out, given time.' And indeed I did – while my friend continued silently to enjoy the spring morning, which was, I fancy, his whole purpose in distracting me!

40. The Priory School

*We had come on a small black ribbon of pathway. In the
middle of it, clearly marked on the sodden soil, was the track of
a bicycle.*
'Hurrah!' I cried. 'We have it.'
*But Holmes was shaking his head, and his face was puzzled
and expectant rather than joyous.*
*'A bicycle, certainly, but not the bicycle,' said he. 'I am
familiar with forty-two different impressions left by tyres. This,
as you perceive, is a Dunlop, with a patch upon the outer
cover. Heidegger's tyres were Palmer's, leaving longitudinal
stripes. . . . Therefore, it is not Heidegger's track.'*

I CANNOT recollect anything more sudden and startling
than the entrance of Thorneycroft Huxtable, MA,
PhD, etc., upon our small stage in Baker Street. No sooner
had he burst through the door, than he collapsed insensible
upon the bearskin hearthrug.

'Absolute exhaustion,' said I, when I had examined our
patient. And as he recovered, and recounted his story, we
began to understand the misfortune which had brought on
this profound fatigue. The academic was at his wits' end
with worry over the apparent abduction of one of his most
prominent students – Lord Saltire, the only son of the
sixth Duke of Holdernesse, KG, PC ('Half the alphabet,'
said Holmes). Also missing was Heidegger, the German
master, whose bicycle was not to be found at its normal
position in the shed.

So within a quarter of an hour, we found ourselves in a
four-wheeler hurtling towards Euston, from which we
would catch the train up into the cold, bracing atmosphere

of the Peak country, in which Dr Huxtable's famous school is situated.

By close examination of the tracks leading from the school across the moors, Holmes was able to reconstruct the events of that fateful night. The abduction mystery turned into a murder enquiry, however, when we discovered the body of a tall, bespectacled man, evincing a frightful blow upon the head, which had crushed in part of his skull. He wore shoes, but no socks, and his open coat disclosed a nightshirt beneath it. This was undoubtedly the body of Heidegger.

I need hardly say that Holmes excelled himself in following the tangled threads of this strange and remarkable business – though even he was astonished by what we heard subsequently from the lips of Lord Holdernesse himself as the full truth of the matter was finally revealed.

Anyway, as we were speeding our way northward to begin our investigation, Dr Huxtable continued to be in a state of considerable nervous agitation. As Holmes drew himself up and puffed on his pipe and mulled over the known facts of the case, I tried to pacify the schoolman by telling him how my friend could be relied upon in such cases, as he had shown in the Darlington substitution scandal. Once his nerves were more calm, I was even able to divert him with one of the little enigmas with which my friend had so often diverted me.

'Here's something appropriate to a case concerning a schoolman,' I said, and handed Huxtable a slip of paper on which I had written the following items:

DOG (   ) SON

TRY (   ) AID

CAP (   ) RED

'Two letters placed inside each set of brackets,' I explained, 'will create other words when placed at the end of the word to the left and the beginning of the word to the right of those same brackets. When you have completed this exercise, you will find that another word can be read downwards. What do you suppose that word to be?'

By the time Huxtable had solved the riddle – of course, it was an old one which I had been given my Holmes much earlier – he seemed to have regained at least some of his normal composure.

41. Black Peter

'I know your methods, sir, and I applied them . . . I examined most carefully the ground outside, and also the floor of the room. There were no footmarks.'

'Meaning that you saw none?'

'I assure you, sir, that there were none.'

'My good Hopkins, I have investigated many crimes, but I have never yet seen one which was committed by a flying creature. As long as the criminal remains upon two legs so long must there be some indentation, some abrasion, some trifling displacement which can be detected by the scientific searcher. It is incredible that this blood-bespattered room contained no trace which could have aided us. I understand, however, from the inquest that there were some objects which you failed to overlook?'

The young inspector winced at my companion's ironical comments.

NO RECORD of the doings of Mr Sherlock Holmes would be complete if it did not include some account of the very unusual affair of '95 concerning the obscure circumstances which surrounded the death of Captain Peter Carey.

The first I knew of this case was when Holmes strode into the room with a huge barbed-headed spear under his arm. He said that he had been attempting to stab a dead pig down at Allardyce's, the butcher-shop: 'And I have satisfied myself,' he continued, 'that by no exertion of my strength can I transfix the pig with a single blow.' And a man's life would depend on that fact.

The young police inspector, Stanley Hopkins, explained the details of the case to me. Captain Peter Carey, once a daring and successful seal- and whale-fisher, had been found dead in the outhouse at his retirement home near Forest Row in Sussex. Right through his broad breast a steel harpoon had been driven, and it had sunk deep into the wood of the wall behind him. The only obvious clue to the identity of the murderer was a drab-covered note-book bearing the initials 'J.H.N.' and the date '1883' on the first page.

Holmes directed Hopkins to call a four-wheeler, and within a quarter of an hour the three of us had started off for Forest Row.

There we found signs that someone had been tampering with the door of the outhouse since Hopkins had last examined it, but had not been able to gain entry. Holmes speculated that the intended burglar would probably return again that night, with stronger tools, and that we could advance the case if we were to lie in wait and apprehend him.

We did indeed apprehend someone: John Hopley

Neligan, whose presence at the scene of the crime late at night, and whose initials, threw him under immediate suspicion; though Holmes remained far from satisfied as to his guilt.

It was a long and melancholy vigil which we settled down to at eleven o'clock. As time wore on our silence became more and more absolute; but in the early minutes the Inspector and I amused ourselves with some whispered challenges back and forth as Holmes's keen senses stayed on alert for our quarry.

'Inspector,' said I, 'here is a little nautical problem which came to me a while ago as I was thinking about this case.' Holmes snorted; most probably in the certain knowledge that I was about to unveil one of his own compositions from the time when we were investigating another seafaring mystery, the loss of the British bark *Sophie Anderson* (or was it that shocking affair of the Dutch steamship *Friesland*?).

'Suppose a steamship is battling against the tide in order to reach its harbour, which is 25 nautical miles away,' I went on, undeterred. 'Its boiler consumes 12 hundredweight of coal every hour and in normal circumstances, with a calm sea and no tide, it would steam along at 8 knots.'

'That is, 8 nautical miles per hour?' asked the Inspector.

'Precisely so,' I confirmed. 'Eight nautical miles per hour. But then suppose that today the tidal flow against it is 1 knot – 1 nautical mile per hour – and it has only 42 hundredweight of fuel on board. Will it reach its harbour?'

'Now,' said the Inspector, 'that's a tricky problem.'

My friend snorted his obvious contempt and continued his vigil.

42. Charles Augustus Milverton

'Criminals?' said Holmes. 'Plural?'
'Yes, there were two of them. They were as nearly as
possible captured red-handed. We have their footmarks, we
have their description, it's ten to one that we trace them. The
first fellow was a bit too active, but the second was caught by
the under-gardener, and only got away after a struggle. He was
a middle-sized, strongly built man – square jaw, thick neck,
moustache, a mask over his eyes.'
'That's rather vague,' said Sherlock Holmes. 'Why, it might
be a description of Watson!'
'It's true,' said the Inspector, with amusement. 'It might be
a description of Watson.'

CHARLES AUGUSTUS Milverton, according to my friend Sherlock Holmes, was 'the king of all the blackmailers' and a singularly odious personage.

'Do you feel a creeping, shrinking sensation, Watson,' he asked me, 'when you stand before the serpents in the Zoo, and see the slithery, gliding, venomous creatures . . . ? Well, that's how Milverton impresses me.'

I was soon to share that creeping sensation, brought on by our adversary when his stately carriage and pair drew up in the street below. A footman opened the door, and a small, stout man in a shaggy astrakhan overcoat descended. A minute later he was in the room.

Holmes had been engaged by an illustrious client to save the fate of the Lady Eva Blackwell, the most beautiful debutante of the previous season, who was due to be married in a fortnight to the Earl of Dovercourt. But Milverton had intercepted some letters to another man which it was clear would bring the proposed match to a very sudden end.

It was a case in which Sherlock Holmes would use his remarkable abilities at disguise to familiarize himself with the layout and workings of Milverton's home establishment. It involved us in an expedition of no little danger, in which we only narrowly escaped being apprehended by the forces of the law; and the outcome, though tragic, brought at least some comfort to the many people of wealth and position who had found themselves compromised by the methodical tortures of Charles Augustus Milverton.

After the case was over and we had recovered from our dangerous excursion, we were breakfasting and mulling over the whole extraordinary episode.

'I discovered, from leafing through that odious Milverton's account book,' said Holmes, 'that in one year alone he made 3010 guineas by selling a number of letters.'

'How much did he sell them for?' I enquired.

'They were all the same price, Watson – which was more than 200 guineas and less than 300 guineas.'

'And how many letters did he sell at this price?'

'Really, Watson!' exclaimed my friend. 'Can't you even work out *that* simple sum?'

43. The Six Napoleons

'But I wish to call your attention very particularly to the
position of this house, in the garden of which the bust was
destroyed.'
Lestrade looked about him.
'It was an empty house, and so he knew that he would not
be disturbed in the garden.'
'Yes, but there is another empty house farther up the street
which he must have passed before he came to this one. Why did
he not break it there, since it is evident that every yard he
carried it increased the risk of someone meeting him?'
'I give it up,' said Lestrade.
Holmes pointed to the street lamp above our heads.
'He could see what he was doing here, and he could not
there. That was his reason.'

INSPECTOR LESTRADE, of Scotland Yard, was at first
reluctant to recount the curious fate that had befallen a
number of busts of Napoleon in recent days. It seemed
altogether too trivial and eccentric to justify the interest of
The Great Detective.

Could it be anything more than a madman who had
acquired such a hatred of Napoleon that he had decided to
smash every known likeness of the emperor all of a sudden?
Indeed, that he would commit burglary to get at them, and
then leave them smashed?

But then it seemed that our madman was prepared to go
even further. At the site of the fourth incident involving a
bust of Napoleon, an unidentified man was found on the
doorstep, a great gash in his throat and the whole place

swimming in blood; though he could not have been the burglar, because the Napoleon itself was found, smashed, a good deal further down the street.

Holmes and I began our investigation by driving down from Kensington to the establishment of the picture-dealer Mr Morse Hudson, of the Kennington Road, a peppery-mannered man who seemed to be the original source for all of the fractured statues.

It was a drive of about an hour. I knew that Holmes thought he had probably uncovered sufficient clues already to work his way to the solution of these strange crimes, because he was surprisingly willing to engage me in conversation as we rattled through the streets of the capital.

'I have a mind to give that peppery shopkeeper a piece of advice,' said my friend. And he stopped at the nearest telegraph-office to dash off a wire directed to Mr Morse Hudson. This is how it ran:

THGI   RSYA   WLAS

IREM   OTSU   CEHT

'That should keep him occupied for a while, don't you think, Watson?'

'I have no doubt about it, Holmes,' I replied. 'But whatever does it mean?'

44. The Three Students

'Surely there is another alternative, Mr Holmes. I don't know
whether you observed my bedroom window?'
'Lattice-paned, lead framework, three separate windows,
one swinging on hinge, and large enough to admit a man.'
'Exactly . . .'

I N THE YEAR of '95, a combination of events caused Mr
Sherlock Holmes and myself to spend some weeks on a
criminal investigation in one of our great university towns.

We were residing at the time in furnished lodgings close
to a library where Sherlock Holmes was pursuing some
laborious researches, when we received a visit from an
acquaintance, Mr Hilton Soames, tutor and lecturer at the
College of St Luke's, which was to lead us off on an entirely
different sort of enquiry.

Mr Soames had left his room for a short time, and
returned to find the door open, with the key in the lock,
and the proofs of the examination papers scattered.

But the intruder had left other traces of his presence
besides the rumpled papers. On the table in the window
were several shreds from a sharpened pencil, and a broken
tip of lead; there was a long cut in the writing-table; and a
small ball of black dough or clay was found alongside.

Three students were under suspicion, since only they
lived in the same part of the building and could have had
access to the tutor's study. Holmes interviewed them all,
and afterwards was able to provide a complete explanation
of the case, which led to the voluntary departure of one of
the students.

But as you can imagine, before this case started to

occupy Holmes's time, our visit to this quaint old town afforded us plenty of opportunities to take some relaxing and educational expeditions through the narrow streets of the university district. It was on one of these rambles that Holmes put to me the following little enigma.

'Why, Watson, here is the 'varsity cricket ground! Tell me, if the average number of runs scored over the first 5 innings of a match is 16, but then after a further 4 innings the average score has risen to 24, what then is the average number of runs scored over the last 4 innings?'

'Sounds like a very long match, Holmes.'

'Quite so, Watson,' he replied curtly, 'but your answer will come very much more quickly, will it not?'

45. The Golden Pince-nez

Sherlock Holmes took the glasses into his hand, and examined them with the utmost attention and interest. He held them on his nose, endeavoured to read through them, went to the window and stared up the street with them, looked at them most minutely in the full light of the lamp, and finally, with a chuckle, seated himself at the table and wrote a few lines upon a sheet of paper, which he tossed across to Stanley Hopkins.

'That's the best I can do for you,' said he. 'It may prove of some use.'

The astonished detective read the note aloud. It ran as follows:

Wanted, a woman of good address, attired like a
lady. She has a remarkably thick nose, with eyes
which are set close upon either side of it. She has a
puckered forehead, a peering expression, and
probably rounded shoulders. There are indications
that she has had recourse to an optician at least
twice during the last few months. As her glasses are
of remarkable strength, and as opticians are not very
numerous, there should be no difficulty in tracing
her.

S O MUCH OF our work for the year 1894 would furnish
a narrative, but none unites so many singular features
as the episode of Yoxley Old Place, which includes the
lamentable death of young Willoughby Smith, and those
subsequent developments which threw so curious a light
upon the causes of the crime.

It was a wild, tempestuous November night that young
Stanley Hopkins, the promising detective, braved in order
to seek my friend's advice.

Mr Willoughby Smith had been engaged as a researcher
and secretary by Professor Coram of Yoxley Old Place in
Kent. It was here that the maid, Susan Tarlton, heard
from downstairs a wild, hoarse scream, strange and unnatural. She opened the study door to find young Smith
stretched upon the floor, fatally stabbed by the professor's
sealing-wax knife, with just enough breath in him to give
the enigmatic clue: 'The professor – it was she.'

But the chair-bound professor was still in his night-
clothes in bed. And it was clear that none of the other
servants were involved.

The only other clue was a golden pince-nez that was
found clasped in the dead man's right hand, obviously
snatched from the face or the person of the assassin.

The solution to this curious case rested on a number of Holmes's observations, including the tracks on the garden path and the fact that the professor's corridor and the back door passage were both lined with coconut matting.

Holmes interviewed Coram – during which time he smoked an unusually large number of the professor's Alexandrian cigarettes – before stepping out into the garden and declaring that nothing more could be done before two o'clock. So we loitered the remainder of the morning away in the garden, and as so often happened at these times of waiting, my friend amused himself by setting me one of his notorious brain-teasers.

'This place makes me think, Watson. The following groups of letters have lost their vowels. Insert the appropriate vowels and find four associated words, one of which can be regarded as odd. What do you suppose that word to be?'

And, tearing a leaf from his pocket-book, he presented me with the following strings of letters:

LPT   BRTT   DDFFL   CCRS

46. The Missing Three-quarter

'We have only to find to whom that telegram is addressed,' I suggested.
'Exactly, my dear Watson. Your reflection, though

profound, had already crossed my mind. But I daresay it may
have come to your notice that, if you walk into a post-office
and demand to see the counterfoil of another man's message,
there may be some disinclination on the part of the officials to
oblige you. There is so much red tape in these matters.
However, I have no doubt that with a little delicacy and finesse
the end may be attained.'

RUGBY FOOTBALL was not a game which impinged upon the world of Mr Sherlock Holmes. So when Godfrey Staunton went missing just before the crucial Oxford–Cambridge match, he had to confess that he had never heard of the crack three-quarter and hero of Cambridge, Blackheath, and five Internationals.

The case interested him, though, and it took a more sinister turn when Holmes established that Staunton had dispatched a telegram just a few hours prior to his disappearance, and of which the closing words had been 'Stand by us for God's sake.'

This was the point at which I made my rather obvious remark about the desirability of tracing the person to whom the telegram was addressed, and had to endure Holmes's riposte about the practical difficulty of such an enterprise. ('I had seven different schemes for getting a glimpse of that telegram, but I could hardly hope to succeed the very first time,' he confided to me after he had done just that.)

It was an adventure which took us to Cambridge and involved the systematic following of a doctor, the employment of one of the local draghounds, and the eventual discovery of our quarry in the most tragic and unfortunate of circumstances.

And so we set off for the old university city. It was already dark when we reached our destination. On the

He turned over the pages lazily.

way, we got to talking about our respective college days, and Holmes explained that he had been something of an athlete too.

'In a 400-yard race once,' he explained, 'I remember beating a fellow student, James Warburton – his father was the victim in that shocking case involving a scheme to induce madness – by 20 yards. So I suggested that we should run the race again, with me starting this time from a point 21 yards behind the starting line.'

'That seems a fair difference.'

'Warburton thought so too, and agreed. Who then do you suppose won the race that time?'

47. The Abbey Grange

'As a matter of fact, that screw was not used. This bottle was opened by a pocket screw, probably contained in a knife, and not more than an inch and a half long. If you will examine the top of the cork, you will observe that the screw was driven in three times before the cork was extracted. It has never been transfixed. The long screw would have transfixed it and drawn it up with a single pull. When you catch this fellow, you will find that he has one of these multiplex knives in his possession.'

'COME, WATSON, come! The game is afoot.' Those were the words to which I awoke one frosty morning towards the end of the winter of '97, just a few minutes before I found Holmes and myself rattling through the silent streets on our way to Charing Cross Station and then down to the Abbey Grange, in Marsham, Kent.

The detective Stanley Hopkins had summoned us once again. Sir Eustace Brackenstall had been found dead, his head knocked in with a poker. Lady Brackenstall was nursing some minor injuries to her own person.

She recounted that, when checking the security of the house the night before, she had found the window of the dining-room open and was suddenly confronted by three intruders, who pulled down the bell-sash and tied her to a chair. Sir Eustace, alarmed by the commotion, came down and rushed at the men, but was overcome and given the fatal blow.

Holmes was able, by close examination of the chair, the bell-sash, some wine-glasses found on the sideboard, and other parts of the room, to discern that the sequence of events was in fact materially different; and strange indeed was the story that came to be told about this unhappy household.

Holmes's acute senses were already racing as we made our way to Chislehurst station, though I was still hardly awake. In an attempt to enliven me, as we drove the couple of miles through those narrow country lanes to the park gate of the Abbey Grange, he brought up one of his favourite sorts of conundrum.

'Perk up, Watson!' said he. 'Tell me what number comes next in this string: 5, 3, 10, 5, 15, 9, 20, 17, 25, . . . ?'

48. The Second Stain

'And yet the motives of women are so inscrutable. You remember the woman at Margate whom I suspected for the same reason. No powder on her nose – that proved to be the correct solution. How can you build on such a quicksand? Their most trivial action may mean volumes, or their most extraordinary conduct may depend upon a hairpin or a curling tongs. Good-morning, Watson.'

THE ADVENTURE of the Second Stain brought not just one, but two visitors of European fame within the walls of our humble room in Baker Street. One was the eagle-eyed Lord Bellinger, twice Premier of Britain; the other was the country's most rising statesman, the Right Honourable Trelawney Hope, Secretary for European Affairs.

A foreign potentate had written a letter of such importance, and of such indiscretion, that its discovery by the wrong hands could certainly have precipitated a European war. And yet this same letter, entrusted to Mr Trelawney Hope, had now gone missing – despite being locked in his despatch-box, secure in his bedroom at home.

Holmes quickly identified the few individuals whom he knew to be capable of a criminal enterprise of such a sort. 'There are only those three capable of playing so bold a game,' he told me. 'There are Oberstein, La Rothiere, and Eduardo Lucas.'

But the tale became even more intricate when I glanced just then at my morning paper, to learn that Eduardo Lucas had been murdered at his home in Godolphin Street that very night. A coincidence? No. 'The odds are enormous against its being coincidence,' reasoned my friend. 'No figures could express them. No, my dear Watson, the two events are connected – *must* be connected.'

This is not the place to explain how Holmes recovered the document by noting that poor Lucas's bloodstain on the carpet in his home did not match the stain on the floor underneath; and how he was able to identify the person who had carried off the letter and arrange for its safe return – much to the relief of our distinguished clients.

But it was a long investigation, spread over several days. I knew that Holmes was keeping in close touch with every development, though if he knew more than appeared in the papers, he kept his own counsel. Still, that was not unusual when he was processing the details of a particularly intricate and sensitive case.

For three mornings things stood like this, with us discussing various subjects in our customary way, but keeping away from the subject of the scandal. We would fill in some time at our breakfast table with desultory chat, or sometimes the analysis of various conundrums that had occurred to one or other of us. One such that I recall was this.

'Two notorious spies have been touring quite a number of countries in the last year, Watson. Carlos, for example, has paid visits to China, Sardinia, Corfu, Finland, Mongolia and Mississippi. David has been to Denmark, Malta, Java and India. And of course, he still has another destination to visit.'

'What on earth could that be, Holmes?' I asked. 'Somewhere like New Zealand, perhaps, or Bohemia – or Canada?'

'Well yes, Watson, I certainly expect him to be visiting one of those countries in the near future. Do you know which one? It's simple enough to work out: I will be generous and give you fifteen minutes to calculate it.'

THE VALLEY OF FEAR

49. The Warning

*'The cipher message begins with a large 534, does it not? We
may take it as a working hypothesis that 534 is the particular
page to which the cipher refers. So our book has already
become a large book, which is surely something gained.
What other indications have we as to the nature of this
large book? The next sign is C2. What do you make of
that, Watson?'*

'Chapter the second, no doubt.'

*'Hardly that, Watson. You will, I am sure, agree with me
that if the page be given, the number of the chapter is
immaterial. Also that if page 534 finds us only in the second
chapter, the length of the first one must have been really
intolerable.'*

'Column!' I cried.

'Brilliant, Watson. You are scintillating this morning.'

SHERLOCK HOLMES took the view that the invention
of the electric telegraph and the steamship had made
the world smaller. He listed several cases in which vital
information was received from overseas in time to detect

and bring justice to a criminal. In these arguments I was, unusually for me, the pessimist. I pointed to the greater propensity for crime offered by modern communications.

I referred in particular to the rise of the international criminal, and to the number of cases in which we had encountered a crime whose origin lay overseas, yet whose last act took place within our jurisdiction. *The Sign of Four* had seen theft and terrible revenge enacted on our shores in response to events in India at the time of the mutiny. The case of *The Study in Scarlet* similarly led to revenge in Britain for dastardly crimes committed years earlier in Salt Lake City.

Holmes came round to my view after our adventure of *The Valley of Fear*. It combined the greatest criminal mind of them all, and a story of horrendous murders on an unbelievable scale committed many years previously in a desolate corner of the United States of America.

Our involvement in the story began with a note from one of my companion's low-life informants, Porlock by name. The note was in cipher, and read thus:

534 C2 13 127 36 31 4 17 21 41
DOUGLAS 109 293 5 37 BIRLSTONE
26 BIRLSTONE 9 47 171

Holmes concluded that the cipher referred to a page of a book, but that it was useless until we knew which book. He was very downcast when a second note came from an obviously frightened Porlock, regretting the first note and declining to name the book needed to decode it.

Holmes deduced immediately the hand of Professor Moriarty, in that Porlock's hand was clear and firm in the first note, yet scarcely legible in the second. Someone had frightened him out of his wits, and it was clear to Holmes who it was.

In one of his dazzling displays, my companion was able to deduce that the key volume must be last year's edition of *Whitaker's Almanac*. He decoded the message and found that it read:

> There–is–danger–may–come–very–soon–one–
> Douglas–rich–country–now–at–Birlstone–
> House–Birlstone–confidence–is–pressing

My esteemed friend hardly had time to savour his intellectual triumph when Alex MacDonald of Scotland Yard appeared to tell us that Mr Douglas of Birlstone Manor House had been horribly murdered the previous night.

We set out for Birlstone on the next train. It was hardly surprising, in view of the cryptic message of such foreboding we had just received, that our talk on the journey turned to codes, words and ciphers. Holmes regarded them as good exercise for the mental skills, though I must confess I never saw the point of most of them, even after they were explained to me.

To illustrate some argument he was developing, Holmes wrote the following items in the condensation of the carriage window:

CALPINE

PROSEY

ROCRAMTON

EXHOPIN

'They mean nothing to me, Holmes,' I confessed.

'I do not want their meaning, Watson,' he replied. 'I already know that. I want you to tell me which is the odd one out.'

'But are we not just about to arrive at our station?' I protested.

'We arrive in four minutes. That should be quite sufficient for you to do it!'

However, for all the progress I made it might just as well have been four years.

50. The Tragedy of Birlstone

'But in calling Moriarty a criminal you are uttering libel in the eyes of the law – and there lie the glory and the wonder of it!

The greatest schemer of all time, the organizer of every deviltry, the controlling brain of the underworld, a brain which might have made or marred the destiny of nations – that's the man! But so aloof is he from general suspicion, so immune from criticism, so admirable in his management and self-effacement, that for those very words you have uttered he could hale you to a court and emerge with your year's pension as a solatium for his wounded character.'

AT BIRLSTONE, which lies in North Sussex, Holmes and I learned some of the key facts of the case. The victim, John Douglas, had come to live at the

Manor House after making money in America, perhaps in the California gold fields. He had been found dead, his body horribly disfigured by a double-barrel shotgun, sawn off, and with triggers wired to discharge together. It was a dastardly weapon for a dastardly act. I had not seen worse injuries in Afghanistan.

The Manor House itself was surrounded by a shallow moat, and could only be approached across a drawbridge which was studiously raised every evening. There were four persons in the house in addition to the deceased. Cecil Barker was a friend of Douglas from the American days. Mrs Ivy Douglas, the widow, was there, as were Ames, the butler, and Mrs Allen, the housekeeper.

Barker had heard a muffled report at half-past eleven, and rushed down to find Douglas dead in his dressing-gown, with a candle burning on the table. He it was who had lit the lamp and called the local constabulary. The sergeant deduced that anyone from outside must have entered before six, and then hidden until Douglas came down at the fatal hour. An open window and a bloody footprint on the sill suggested an escape over the moat.

Curious features were a hammer, unmarked, upon the rug, and a crudely lettered card bearing the inscription V.V. – 341. There were muddy bootmarks behind a curtain where the murderer might have waited in hiding. There were two curiosities about the deceased. One was the fact that his wedding ring was gone, even though the ring worn below it was still there. Someone had apparently removed both rings and replaced the other. There was also an utterly strange mark on the victim's arm. It was a triangle inside a circle, and had been not tattooed, but branded years ago. It had often been seen by both wife and butler.

It was all quite beyond me, but my companion set about

these bizarre circumstances with his customary skill. He rapidly equated the letters PSA on the firearm with the Pennsylvania Small Arms Company, indicating a possible American connection. He noticed the small plaster on the victim's jaw, a shaving cut showing possible nervousness that day, a fact confirmed by the butler. Holmes also paid a great deal of attention to the fact that a single dumb-bell was found under the table; only one.

Under questioning Barker reported that when Douglas had left California years earlier, it had been suddenly, and that within a week half a dozen men had arrived asking about him. The widow also reported her husband had been afraid of something called the Valley of Fear, whatever that was.

There were two disturbing things we discovered. First Holmes matched the bloody footprint with Barker's slipper. Clearly it had been faked to create the appearance of exit through the window. Then I chanced to come across Barker and Mrs Douglas unexpectedly. They were smiling and animated, not like a grieving best friend and widow.

When an abandoned bicycle was found, and the police traced it to an unknown stranger named Hargreave who had been seen in Tunbridge Wells, it was too much for me, but Holmes took it in his stride. He falsely put it about that the moat was to be drained, and caught Barker fishing a parcel out of it during the night, a parcel weighted down with the missing dumb-bell.

I remember that, just after noon on that first day when Holmes and I had arrived in Birlstone, we had walked from the Westville Arms down the quaint village street and into the winding drive of the Manor House.

'It will take us a good five minutes to walk up this impressive avenue,' said Holmes. 'Just enough time, Watson, for you to tell me: Which word of three letters can be attached to the front of LAPSE, OUR, LEAGUE and LATE to create four other English words?'

He had challenged me to solve this puzzle within five minutes; in fact I did it in four.

51. The Scowrers

Such were the methods of the Society of Freemen, and such were the deeds of the Scowrers by which they spread their rule of fear over the great and rich district which was for so long a period haunted by their terrible presence. Why should these pages be stained by further crimes? Have I not said enough to show the men and their methods?

These deeds are written in history, and there are records wherein one may read the details of them.

SINCE BARKER and Mrs Douglas failed to explain themselves, my friend – to everyone's astonishment – suggested that Mr Douglas might best tell his own story. Amid general consternation, Jack Douglas himself stepped into the room from his secret hideout.

As Holmes had suspected, it was the man who tried to kill him who had died. He had hidden in wait for Douglas, but in the struggle the gun went off and killed the would-be murderer. Mr and Mrs Douglas, aided by Barker, decided to fake Douglas's death to prevent further plots against him. Holmes had computed it all correctly, and we were rewarded with the enthralling story of the Scowrers, the most evil and murderous bunch I had ever heard of.

It had all started in the hard winter of 1875, in the coal-mining country of Vermissa Valley in the United States. A young man, John McMurdo, arrived in town. It was quickly established that he had been in trouble in Chicago, having engaged in forgery and perhaps murder. He was soon inducted into the local chapter of the Eminent Order of Freemen, Lodge 341.

The Order, which elsewhere was a charity and good fellowship society, was in Vermissa Valley a group with more than fifty murders to its name. In the brutish world of American coal mining, it was a Socialist terror squad which blackmailed and murdered mine-owners, foremen and managers, and anyone who dared speak out against its reign of bloody terror. Its members were known as the Scowrers.

They operated on a mutual aid basis, sending killers to do their work in other pits, and inviting their opposite numbers in to return the favour. This meant that the murders were rarely carried out by men from the immediate locality. At the time McMurdo arrived on the scene, they had gripped the valley with their evil for more than a decade.

McMurdo himself was branded with their sign when he was sworn in. His sturdy independence and loyalty to the Order's head, Bodymaster Black Jack McGinty, helped establish him within the Order, and he was soon participating in their murderous attacks. This strained but did not break his loving relationship with Ettie Shafter, his landlord's daughter.

When McMurdo had progressed to become Inner Deacon of the Order, with every chance of succeeding Bodymaster McGinty, he received a tip-off that a Pinkerton agent, Birdy Edwards, had been hired by the mine-owners back east to put an end to the Scowrers once and

In the old room in Baker Street.

for all. The group was alarmed for the first time at so fearsome an adversary, but agreed to put McGinty in charge of a trap for the fellow. As seven of the top Scowrers prepared for McMurdo to bring Birdy Edwards into their trap, he appeared alone.

After we had heard this strange story, Holmes put to me an intellectual problem which, he remarked, was inspired by the responses by which the Ancient Order of Freemen recognized each other.

'Consider this grid of numbers,' said he, quickly jotting down the following array:

9	4	8	6	7
6	3	7	1	8
8	5	7	7	6
5	4	6	2	7
6	7	5	9	?

'Now, if someone claiming to be a member were presented with such a test, what number would he be expected to supply, in place of the question mark, to make up the square?'

He allowed me eight minutes for my answer; and after that time and more had elapsed, he observed that my failure could have cost me my very life in the Valley of Fear.

52. The Trapping of Birdy Edwards

'Well!' cried Boss McGinty at last. 'Is he here? Is Birdy Edwards here?'
'Yes,' McMurdo answered slowly. 'Birdy Edwards is here. I am Birdy Edwards!'
There were ten seconds after that brief speech during which the room might have been empty, so profound was the silence. The hissing of a kettle upon the stove rose sharp and strident to the ear. Seven white faces, all turned upward to this man who

dominated them, were set motionless with utter terror. Then, with a sudden shivering of glass, a bristle of glistening rifle barrels broke through each window, while the curtains were torn from their hangings.

At the sight Boss McGinty gave the roar of a wounded bear and plunged for the half-opened door. A levelled revolver met him there with the stern blue eyes of Captain Marvin of the mine police gleaming behind the sights. The Boss recoiled and fell back into his chair.

THERE WAS, of course, more to this story of the Scowrers. Having revealed himself as the Pinkerton man, McMurdo – alias Edwards – left town in the early hours with his beloved Ettie, whom he married ten days later. After his testimony at the trial, Boss McGinty and eight henchmen were hanged, with fifty-odd Scowrers imprisoned for various terms.

As the first were released ten years later, they came in vengeance. Edwards and his wife escaped two attempts in Chicago and then fled to California for several years, where his wife died, but where he managed to amass a fortune with his English partner, Barker. Just in time he received warning that his pursuers were on to him, and fled to England, under the name of John Douglas, to marry again and live for five years as a Sussex county gentleman. And this is where Holmes and I, and his relentless pursuers, caught up with him.

He was acquitted on grounds of self-defence, and left the country at once. The story had an unhappy and ominous ending, though. One day Holmes received an unsigned note which said simply, 'Dear me, Mr Holmes. Dear me!'

Holmes was disquieted. 'Deviltry, Watson!' he remarked, and plainly some dark cloud had descended upon him.

His fears proved well founded. Cecil Barker called in to say he had heard from Mrs Douglas that her husband had been lost overboard off St Helena. It appeared to be an accident, but Holmes had no doubt that the tragedy had been stage-managed by Professor Moriarty. The remnants of the Scowrers had obviously engaged him at the first. After the initial failure he had stepped in because he could not be seen to fail.

Barker and I were outraged to see Moriarty apparently get away with this but Holmes, in pensive mood, assured us that he would, given time, bring the brigand to justice.

It was plain that Holmes would be brooding on this for some time. As if to confirm that he wanted to avoid conversation for a while, he scribbled twelve words on a scrap of paper and tossed them over to me. The note read:

NOPOS   **ETER**   **ELIM**

NAWL   **PLEAP**   **ATE**

REWOM   **THILG**   **OTOF**

LIKLER   **HELAW**   **ALBL**

'Solve,' he instructed. 'Eight minutes.'

'But, Holmes!' I exclaimed. 'This is gibberish. ATE is the only real word among them.' Then, reflecting on how our case had started, it dawned on me that they were all in code.

'Not only that,' said Holmes, 'they form into six pairs of words which go together. What are they?'

I had managed to find three of those pairs in the time allotted to me. Too often, as I said, words fail me.

REMINISCENCES OF SHERLOCK HOLMES

53. Wisteria Lodge

'My dear Watson, you know how bored I have been since we locked up Colonel Carruthers. My mind is like a racing engine, tearing itself to pieces because it is not connected up with the work for which it was built. Life is commonplace; the papers are sterile; audacity and romance seem to have passed forever from the criminal world. Can you ask me, then, whether I am ready to look into any new problem, however trivial it may prove? But here, unless I am mistaken, is our client.'

HARDLY HAD Mr Scott Eccles arrived at Baker Street to consult us over what he called a 'most incredible and grotesque experience' than Inspector Gregson of Scotland Yard bustled in to question him about the murder of Mr Aloysius Garcia, of Wisteria Lodge, near Esher. A letter of his had been found in the dead man's pocket, and he admitted that he had passed the night at that very address.

He told us – and the inspector – that he knew Garcia as a Spanish diplomat, and had accepted an invitation to visit. But the house turned out to be an old, tumble-down building, in a state of disrepair. The whole place was depressing, his host seemed distracted, and at eleven he was glad to go to bed.

When he awoke it was broad daylight, and the house was entirely deserted. There was no sign of host, footman, nor cook. Mr Eccles's enquiries revealed that Garcia was unknown at the Spanish embassy. Was it all some absurd practical joke?

The discovery of Garcia's body upon Oxshott Common, nearly a mile from his home, made it clear that there must be some far more sinister explanation to these strange events.

It was nearly six o'clock before we found ourselves in Esher, where we secured comfortable quarters at the Bull. It was a cold March evening, and Holmes and I warmed ourselves at the fire.

'I believe, Watson,' said my friend at last, 'that the exact behaviour of timepieces could be of some material importance to this case. So let me test you upon the subject.' I knew that I was in for another of Holmes's knotty little problems.

'Now, imagine that there are two clocks,' he continued. 'Both were correct at midnight, but then one began to gain at the rate of two and one-quarter minutes every hour. It stopped one and one-half hours ago, showing 8.45 p.m. What time will the second clock be showing now?'

54. The Cardboard Box

*'So much for the string, then,' said Holmes, smiling, 'now for
the box wrapper. Brown paper, with a distinct smell of coffee.
What, did you not observe it? I think there can be no doubt of
it. Address printed in rather straggling characters: "Miss S.
Cushing, Cross Street, Croydon." Done with a broad-pointed
pen, probably a J, and with very inferior ink. The word
"Croydon" has been originally spelled with an "i", which
has been changed to a "y". The parcel was directed, then,
by a man – the printing is distinctly masculine – of limited
education and unacquainted with the town of Croydon. So far,
so good!'*

WHEN A CARDBOARD box containing two severed
human ears packed in salt was delivered to Miss
Susan Cushing of Cross Street, Croydon, Inspector Lestrade wasted little time in calling for the services of my
friend Mr Sherlock Holmes.

So, rising superior to the oppressive summer heat, we
set off for Croydon on the next train. Holmes soon
dismissed Lestrade's pet theory – that some medical students who once lodged at Miss Cushing's house were
playing an ugly trick on her by sending some relics of the
dissecting-room.

'I repeat that there is no practical joke here,' he told us,
after a minute examination of the box, its wrappings and
its grisly contents, 'but that we are investigating a serious
crime.'

The next stage of our investigation took us, via the
telegraph office, to the home of Miss Cushing's sister in
Wallington, about a mile away, where we did not even

gain admittance; but Holmes seemed cheerful none the less and we stopped off for lunch before re-joining Lestrade at the police station.

Here, Holmes astonished us by revealing that he was now able to lay bare every detail of the shocking crime that had been committed! And it would turn out to be a circle of misery and violence and fear, of love and hatred and murder.

As he explained it to me, I understood why he had been so cheerful all through our pleasant little lunch together that day – even though our visit to Wallington had appeared to produce no facts whatsoever.

I have written that he would talk about nothing but violins, and lingered more than an hour over a bottle of claret as he recounted anecdote after anecdote about Paganini. That is not quite true: the intricate patterns of that extraordinary composer's musical creations led him into a brief digression on another complex pattern that had caught his interest earlier.

'Consider this array of figures, Watson! Tell me which number should replace the question mark.'

And on the back of the menu he wrote down a square of figures:

$$
\begin{array}{ccccc}
6 & 1 & 4 & 3 & 7 \\
2 & 5 & 4 & 3 & 1 \\
4 & 3 & 2 & 5 & 5 \\
5 & 2 & 7 & 0 & 4 \\
? & 4 & 1 & 6 & 4 \\
\end{array}
$$

I puzzled it out every way I could. Now *what* exactly could the pattern be?

55. The Red Circle

'The first thing that strikes one is the obvious possibility that the person now in the rooms may be entirely different from the one who engaged them.'
'Why should you think so?'
'Well, apart from this cigarette-end, was it not suggestive that the only time the lodger went out was immediately after his taking the rooms? He came back – or someone else came back – when all witnesses were out of the way. We have no proof that the person who came back was the person who went out. Then, again, the man who took the rooms spoke English well. This other, however, prints "match" when it should have been "matches". I can imagine that the word was taken out of a dictionary, which would give the noun but not the plural. The laconic style may be to conceal the absence of knowledge of English. Yes, Watson, there are good reasons to suspect that there has been a substitution of lodgers.'

MRS WARREN asked fifty shillings a week for the small sitting-room and bedroom at the top of her house in Great Orme Street, near the British Museum. But her lodger had offered twice that sum if he could have it on his own terms – that he was to have a key to the house and would never, upon any excuse, be disturbed.

He went out that same night, returning late; and neither Mrs Warren, her husband, nor the house-girl had seen anything of him since. Food went in, brief handwritten instructions came out; but not once in ten days did anyone catch even a glimpse of the strange lodger on the top floor.

At first my friend was reluctant to engage his mind on the case. But as Mrs Warren's story unfolded, he had to agree that there were certainly some points of interest in it.

Holmes agreed to call upon Mrs Warren at about the time her lodger normally took lunch – a tray was left outside the door – so we had until mid-day before having to set off for our appointment. As always at such times, Holmes seemed pre-occupied with the case and his theories, though having so little to go on thus far, I found it relatively easy to distract him on other subjects that came into my head as I perused the morning papers.

'Here's one I have devised for you, Holmes,' I said proudly as I laid before him a piece of paper on which I had written my little conundrum, thus:

TIGER __ LIKES

BORED __ HOLDS

FOWLS __ HALLS

CAVES __ HONED

BENCH __ PAGAN

'Now,' continued I, 'change the centre letter of each word to the left and each word to the right – '

'Yes, yes,' interjected Holmes, 'using the same letter for each in order to form two other English words. Then put the letter that you have used in the gap between them and read downwards, whereupon we will find that a new word will be formed. Hum!'

'My dear Holmes . . . !'

'I am sorry to be brusque with you, my dear friend,' replied Sherlock Holmes, 'but this so-called problem of yours really is too trivial.' And he paced over to the window to see if something more interesting might be going on *outside*.

56. The Bruce-Partington Plans

'The London criminal is certainly a dull fellow,' said he in the querulous voice of the sportsman whose game has failed him. 'Look out of this window, Watson. See how the figures loom up, are dimly seen, and then blend once more into the cloud-bank. The thief or the murderer could roam London on such a day as the tiger does the jungle, unseen until he pounces, and then evident only to his victim.'

'There have,' said I, 'been numerous petty thefts.'

Holmes snorted his contempt.

IT WOULD take a singularly rare occurrence to precipitate Mr Mycroft Holmes out of his natural orbit between Pall Mall, the Diogenes Club and Whitehall. But this is exactly what happened in late November, 1895.

Sherlock Holmes's older brother had created a unique job for himself, thanks to his remarkable powers – 'the tidiest and most orderly brain, with the greatest capacity for storing facts, of any man living,' according to my friend the detective. The conclusions of every government department would be passed to him, and he would be the central exchange, the clearing-house, which makes out the balance.

The incident which had caused this Jupiter to descend on Baker Street was the discovery of the body of a young man, Arthur Cadogan West, a clerk at Woolwich Arsenal, near an underground line that Tuesday morning. It was widely assumed that he had fallen from a train. But the mystery was intensified by Mycroft's report that the young man had no underground ticket on his person, and that his pocket contained seven of the ten stolen pages of plans for the Bruce-Partington submarine.

After hearing the strange facts of the case, Holmes and I set off, in the company of Inspector Lestrade, to visit the scene of the incident, upon the point where the railway emerges from the tunnel immediately before Aldgate station.

Holmes stood gazing with an expression of strained intensity upon his face, staring at the railway metals where they curved out of the tunnel, and fixing his eager, questioning eyes on the points; though neither Lestrade nor I (nor the red-faced old gentleman from the railway company who had joined us) could see anything at the scene very worthy of such close examination.

As Holmes continued to stare, we asked our old companion how long he had worked with the railway and what other curious occurrences had befallen him in that time. In reply he recalled that, on one occasion, two engines were tested over a 200-yard stretch of track, whereupon the new engine showed that it could beat the old one by 40 yards.

'So we ran the race again,' said the railwayman, 'this

time with the new engine starting 50 yards further back behind the starting line. Both engines ran at the same speed as before, and do you know what the result was this time?'

'Elementary,' said Holmes. 'Anyone with an IQ of 138 – the top 5% of the population, you know, Watson – could solve a question like that quite easily in no more than seven minutes!'

57. The Dying Detective

Mrs Hudson, the landlady of Sherlock Holmes, was a long-suffering woman. Not only was her first-floor flat invaded at all hours by throngs of singular and often undesirable characters but her remarkable lodger showed an eccentricity and irregularity in his life which must have sorely tried her patience. His incredible untidiness, his addiction to music at strange hours, his occasional revolver practice within doors, his weird and often malodorous scientific experiments, and the atmosphere of violence and danger which hung around him made him the very worst tenant in London. On the other hand, his payments were princely.

I N THE DIM light of a foggy November day the gaunt and wasted face of my friend Mr Sherlock Holmes sent a chill to my heart. Nor would he let me come near him because of the awful nature of his complaint, which he described as 'a coolie disease from Sumatra . . . One thing only is certain. It is infallibly deadly, and it is horribly contagious.'

Mycroft Holmes was a much larger and stouter man than Sherlock.

I offered to fetch Dr Ainstree, the greatest living authority on tropical diseases, but he barred me from any such action. Instead he implored me to fetch Mr Culverton Smith of 13 Lower Burke Street, not a medical man, but a planter from Sumatra, and 'the man upon earth who is best versed in this disease', according to my suffering friend.

Suffice it to say that, after the visit of Mr Culverton Smith, Holmes made a complete recovery from his affliction; but not before he had cleared up an extraordinary criminal mystery surrounding Mr Culverton Smith himself.

'I think that something nutritious at Simpson's would not be out of place,' said my emaciated friend when it was all over. And it was with much relief and thanks for his very rapid recovery that I was happy to join him at that famous Strand establishment.

As Holmes lay on his sick-couch, however, raving about oysters and half-crowns, it should have occurred to me that his mind was not as deranged as he intended me to think. Because one string of seemingly random words which he stuttered did (I subsequently realised) have a logical connection.

Over dinner at Simpson's my friend told me that it should have taken me no more than twelve minutes to find the connection between the string of words, which were:

COCOA   PUPPY   ICICLE
LILAC   BUBBLE

58. The Disappearance of Lady Frances Carfax

'By the way, Holmes,' I added, 'I have no doubt the connection between my boots and a Turkish bath is a perfectly self-evident one to a logical mind, and yet I should be obliged to you if you would indicate it.'

'The train of reasoning is not very obscure, Watson,' said Holmes with a mischievous twinkle. 'It belongs to the same elementary class of deduction which I should illustrate if I were to ask you who shared your cab in your drive this morning.'

'I MUCH FEAR that some evil has come to the Lady Frances Carfax,' exclaimed Holmes. The sole survivor of the Earl of Rufton's family, she had last been heard of at the Hotel National at Lausanne, and then seemingly disappeared without trace.

Holmes was engaged on a particularly critical case in London, so I was dispatched to Lausanne to find out more. There I discovered that Lady Frances's luggage had been forwarded to Baden. At that spa I picked up her trail again at the Englischer Hof, where she had stayed for a fortnight and had made the acquaintance of a Dr Schlessinger and his wife, a missionary from South America. Then the three of them had set off together for London, and nothing had been heard of them since.

I telegraphed Holmes to tell him of the progress I was making, only to find his reply asked me for a description of Dr Schlessinger's left ear. I took no notice of this ill-timed jest – until Holmes himself arrived on the scene to chide me for making a hash of the whole investigation, and took me straight back to London by the night express.

As we sat opposite each other in the gloomy carriage, I could see that Holmes was still nurturing a silent anger concerning my stumbling efforts. But he was still not in a mood to discuss the case until he had more data to work on. For a while I tried to distract him with small-talk about the sights and sounds of the southern European country-side, but he broke sharply into my idle chatter.

'Let me tell you about another little disappearance, Watson,' said he, scribbling some letters on the back of his ticket. 'A missing word, the location of which is not immediately obvious.' I looked at the ticket, on which he had written:

A C   I B
H L   V E

N S   R E
D T   O K

'Select two letters from each square,' he continued. 'Once the correct eight letters have been chosen, a hidden word will be revealed. What is the word?'

59. The Devil's Foot

'I had got as far as Plymouth upon my way to Africa, but the news reached me this morning, and I came straight back again to help in the inquiry.'

Holmes raised his eyebrows.

'Did you lose your boat through it?'

'I will take the next.'

'Dear me! that is friendship indeed.'

'I tell you they were relatives.'

'Quite so – cousins of your mother. Was your baggage aboard the ship?'

'Some of it, but the main part at the hotel.'

'I see. But surely this event could not have found its way into the Plymouth morning papers.'

'No, sir, I had a telegram.'

'May I ask from whom?'

A shadow passed over the gaunt face of the explorer.

'You are very inquisitive, Mr Holmes.'

'It is my business.'

'**W**HY NOT tell them of the Cornish horror – strangest case I have handled.' That was the content of the telegram (Holmes would never write a letter where a telegram would suffice) that made me pick up my pen to write that most curious tale, the Adventure of the Devil's Foot.

In March 1897, Holmes's iron constitution was bending under the strain of constant hard work, and he was ordered to surrender himself to a period of total rest. So for a complete change of air and scenery, we took a small cottage near the windswept Poldhu Bay in Cornwall.

Here Holmes immersed himself into some speculations about the roots of the ancient Cornish language, and spent much of his time in long walks upon the moor. But our peace was shattered early on Tuesday, March the 16th, when the vicar of the parish, Mr Roundhay, and his tenant, Mr Mortimer Tregennis, burst in on us in a very agitated state.

Mr Tregennis had left his sister and two brothers on the Monday night, happily playing cards at their home in Tredannick Wartha. But on the Tuesday morning, the sister was found dead, while the brothers were raving with the senses stricken clean out of them.

'I will look into this matter,' said my friend. 'I confess that I have seldom known a case which at first sight presented a more singular problem.'

But the case would become even more sinister when, the next night, Mr Mortimer Tregennis himself was found dead, and with exactly the same symptoms as the rest of his family.

As Holmes cleared his mind to make sense of this strange case, he and I took a walk along the cliffs, searching for flint arrows, which, he suggested, we were more likely to find than clues to the problem.

'Fat tramp curses John!' he exclaimed, quite without warning.

'Holmes! Is something wrong? Whatever can you mean?' I honestly thought that the strain of overwork had temporarily affected my friend's mind.

'Oh, nothing, Watson,' he reassured me. 'It is just a way of helping me remember what clothing I must pack on an overseas trip that I must make shortly – '

'Holmes! You really do need a rest!'

'I understand your concern, Doctor,' he continued, 'but it is an excursion made necessary by a case of some international sensitivity and importance, and to which I must return *after* this little rest-cure you have devised for me.'

'Well, I cannot say that I approve. But even so, how on earth can that nonsense help you remember what to pack?' I enquired, quite befuddled.

'Simple, Watson. When you unscramble the letters of FAT TRAMP CURSES JOHN, you will find the three items of clothing that I must remember to take. Surely you can see instantly what those items of clothing must be?'

60. His Last Bow

'Good old Watson! You are the one fixed point in a changing age. There's an east wind coming all the same, such a wind as never blew on England yet. It will be cold and bitter, Watson, and a good many of us may wither before its blast. But it's God's own wind nonetheless, and a cleaner, better, stronger land will lie in the sunshine when the storm has cleared. Start her up, Watson, for it's time that we were on our way.'

IT WAS AUGUST 1914, and Von Bork – a man who could hardly be matched among all the devoted agents of the Kaiser – needed just one more document to complete his meticulous collection of British defence secrets.

As the lights of Harwich twinkled in the distance, his Irish-American informant drew up in a small car, carrying the last element – an index of every last naval code, semaphore, lamp code, Marconi . . .

The tall, gaunt visitor betrayed some agitation. Others

of the German's informants had been arrested recently. Was he giving away his own agents? There was some argument: but soon Von Bork had exchanged a cheque of £500 for the brown paper parcel carried by the other.

I shall not recount here how Sherlock Holmes exposed the treachery of this German who played the sporting, devil-may-care young country squire, nor the modest part which I played in the affair; for that has been done elsewhere.

But when I recall this sensational case, there always sticks in my mind a singular little question with which, said my friend, he once ascertained that another seeming English gentleman was in fact a continental spy.

'Any Englishman who claims high intelligence should be able to identify which of these numbers is the odd one out, within about ten minutes,' he explained. And he wrote down the pattern for me, thus:

20	26	23	2
29	3	13	24
27	25	17	10
22	12	21	28

THE CASE BOOK OF SHERLOCK HOLMES

61. The Illustrious Client

*Colonel Damery threw up his kid-gloved hands with a laugh.
'There is no getting past you, Mr Holmes! So you have already
sized him up as a murderer?'*

*'It is my business to follow the details of Continental crime.
Who could possibly have read what happened at Prague and
have any doubts as to the man's guilt! It was a purely technical
legal point and the suspicious death of a witness that saved him!
I am as sure that he killed his wife when the so-called
"accident" happened in the Splugen Pass as if I had seen him
do it. I knew, also, that he had come to England and had a
presentiment that sooner or later he would find me some work
to do. Well, what has Baron Gruner been up to?'*

O N 3 SEPTEMBER 1902, Holmes and I were relaxing
on our couches in the Northumberland Avenue
Turkish baths, when he revealed to me that Sir James
Damery – a man with a reputation for arranging delicate

matters which are to be kept out of the papers – would be calling upon us that afternoon, on a matter he described as 'very delicate' in nature.

Sharp to the time, Sir James appeared in Baker Street, to explain that Violet de Merville, daughter of the illustrious general, had become romantically entangled with the scheming Baron Adelbert Gruner. No appeals from her family would disengage her. Could the powers of Sherlock Holmes help?

The resolution of this affair, and the exposure of the Baron's dark secrets and the catalogue of other souls he had ruined, led us to some strange folk and into some strange events. Indeed, at one point I had to become an expert on antique Chinese porcelain.

Holmes visited Miss de Merville, and the Baron. But for his pains he was rewarded only with rejection and with threats – which subsequently developed into a murderous attack upon his person, much reported in the newspapers.

Anyway, as we idled away in Northumberland Avenue, all this was in front of us and our minds were, for the moment, clear of any such adventure. And Holmes, gazing up at the mosaic ceilings, toyed casually with some of the little problems with which he liked to tease me occasionally.

'Regarding one of the English baths in this place,' he told me, ' – and you know, Watson, that a good English bath is much to be preferred over this Turkish variety – I have made some interesting observations.

'When the plug is in,' he continued, 'one tap will fill the bath in 7 minutes. The other tap is much faster, and will fill it in only 3 minutes. The bath, from when it is full, takes 2 minutes to drain dry after the plug is pulled.'

'When both taps are off, you mean?'

'Yes, of course, Watson, when both taps are off. But that is the question – how long do you think the bath would take to fill, from empty, with the plug out and both taps running? That should amuse you for a while.' And indeed it did.

62. The Blanched Soldier

'From South Africa, sir, I perceive.'

'Yes sir,' he answered, with some surprise.

'Imperial Yeomanry, I fancy.'

'Exactly.'

'Middlesex Corps, no doubt.'

'That is so. Mr Holmes, you are a wizard.'

I smiled at his bewildered expression.

'When a gentleman of virile appearance enters my room with such tan upon his face as an English sun could never give, and with his handkerchief in his sleeve instead of his pocket, it is not difficult to place him. You wear a short beard, which shows you were not a regular. You have the cut of a riding-man. As to Middlesex, your card has already shown me that you are a stock-broker from Throgmorton Street. What other regiment would you join?'

IT WAS JANUARY 1903 when this veteran of the Boer War, Mr James Dodd, called at Baker Street to relate the singular circumstances surrounding the disappearance of his old comrade-in-arms, Godfrey Emsworth, son of Colonel Emsworth, the distinguished Crimean VC.

And now, with the war over and everyone back home, Dodd wrote to the Colonel to ask where Godfrey might be found: but received only the brush-off that he had gone on a year-long voyage round the world. This behaviour seemed unnatural, since it was unlike Godfrey to depart on so long a trip without informing his old friends. So Dodd set off for the family home of Tuxbury Old Park, near Bedford, to investigate for himself.

There he was received with some hostility by Colonel Emsworth, who would not even tell him when and on what line Godfrey had departed upon this long voyage. But later he thought that he caught sight of Godfrey in a locked outhouse, guarded by some second man. Immediately upon his discovery, the colonel put him on a trap with instructions that he was to catch the next train back to London.

What could it all mean? Holmes found the case of some little interest, and elected to return with our visitor to see what more could be discovered at Tuxbury Old Park.

As we drove to Euston we picked up an old friend of his – a gentleman of iron-gray aspect, whom Holmes said might be important in the case.

As usual at such times, Holmes wasted no words throughout the railway journey, and his gray friend remained grave and taciturn. But Mr Dodd was keen to talk about his strange experiences and, as Holmes sat in silence, succeeded in engaging the other in some small-talk.

'Sir,' said he, 'this slightly inclement weather makes me think of an interesting puzzle I picked up during my service overseas.'

And with his finger he drew the following diagram on the steamy window of the carriage.

'If you start at the centre R in this diagram,' he continued, 'and move to adjacent letters, collecting four letters each time – then how many different ways are there of collecting the letters of the word RAIN?'

'Can I move diagonally?' asked the other. 'And does a reversed route count one, or two?'

'No,' said Dodd, 'you cannot move diagonally. But yes, I will give you two for a reversed route. Now try it. We are only five minutes away from the station – you should be able to do it in that time.' And our taciturn acquaintance succeeded in doing precisely that.

63. The Mazarin Stone

'You have not, I hope, learned to despise my pipe and my lamentable tobacco? It has to take the place of food these days.'
'But why not eat?'

'Because the faculties become refined when you starve them. Why, surely, as a doctor, my dear Watson, you must admit that what your digestion gains in the way of blood supply is so much lost to the brain. I am a brain, Watson. The rest of me is a mere appendix. Therefore, it is the brain I must consider.'

PLAINLY I HAD returned to my old quarters at a critical moment. Holmes announced that he expected to be murdered that very evening – and gave me not only the name, but the exact address of the intending perpetrator.

But why not have the criminal arrested immediately? Because, said Holmes, the famous Mazarin Stone – that great yellow crown-jewel recently purloined in a sensational hundred-thousand-pound burglary – had not yet been recovered. Only the one who planned Holmes's demise could reveal its whereabouts.

Just then, Billy came in to announce the arrival of that self-same villain whose name Holmes had given me – Count Negretto Sylvius. Holmes despatched me to Scotland Yard to fetch Youghal of the Criminal Investigation Department, and sent Billy down to the waiting-room to show his adversary upstairs.

The big, swarthy fellow, a famous game-shot and sportsman, entered the room, to see the figure of Mr Sherlock Holmes in an armchair, face turned three-quarters to the window, head down as if reading. It was too good an opportunity to miss. He raised his thick stick, crouching to administer the final blow, when . . .

Well, I should be giving away too much of the story if I recounted here exactly how Holmes escaped from such a seemingly mortal strike. But those who remember the Adventure of the Empty House, and the remarkable skills of the Frenchman Tavernier, may well be able to guess the solution. Let me say no more than to record with satisfaction that the episode ended with the arrest of the Count and his accomplice, the return of the Mazarin Stone, and the safe survival of my friend Sherlock Holmes.

'Our good friend seemed to think he had experienced a ------- when he had managed to ------- his lost jewel,' said Holmes at this point, after it was all over.

'What on earth do you mean, Holmes?' said I. Given the personal danger that Holmes had been in, and the psychological pressure that had been weighing on him, I thought for an instant that my friend had temporarily lost control of his senses. My expression must have betrayed this to The Great Detective.

'No need to look so quizzical, Watson,' said he. 'Simply a little jest. You see, you can replace the blanks in my sentence with two words, which use the same seven letters in their construction. When you have worked out the correct letters, the meaning of my sentence will be abundantly clear to you.'

64. The Three Gables

'Of course, when people bury treasure nowadays they do it in the Post-Office bank. But there are always some lunatics about. It would be a dull world without them. At first I thought of some buried valuable. But why, in that case, should they want your furniture? You don't happen to have a Raphael or a first folio Shakespeare without knowing it?'
'No, I don't think I have anything rarer than a Crown Derby tea-set.'

'That would hardly justify all this mystery. Besides, why should they not openly state what they want? If they covet your tea-set, they can surely offer a price for it without buying you out, lock, stock, and barrel. No, as I read it, there is something which you do not know that you have, and which you would not give up if you did know.'

'That is how I read it,' said I.

'Dr Watson agrees, so that settles it.'

THE ADVENTURE of the Three Gables opened as dramatically and abruptly as any I recall. A huge negro man burst into the room, ordered my friend to keep out of 'other folks' business' and very openly threatened physical violence if he did not.

But our intruder was surprised when Holmes was able to give his name (Steve Dixie) and that of his accomplice (Barney Stockdale) – and to recall some past events which the bruiser would perhaps prefer were not reported to the police. This information quite turned the tables, and after a spluttering apology our visitor bolted out of the room almost as precipitately as he had entered.

It was this incident that decided Holmes to look into the case of Mrs Mary Maberley, of The Three Gables near Harrow Weald, with which he knew the intimidating visit was concerned. A short railway journey, and an even shorter drive, brought us to the house.

It transpired that three days earlier, Mrs Maberley had a call from a man who said that he was a house agent, and that he had a client who would purchase the house for a handsome sum – provided that every item in it was included also. The request seemed so odd that she had asked the advice of my friend.

Holmes reasoned – and I agreed – that there must be something in the house of which Mrs Maberley was unaware, and for which the intending purchaser would part with a very great sum of money. He advised that all the packing-cases containing the effects of her son Douglas, who had recently died of pneumonia in Rome, should be taken upstairs and that her lawyer should be asked to stay in the house as a protection.

Alas, Mrs Maberley did not take the advice, and her house was burgled that very night. Her son's effects had been ransacked; the only clue was a shred of manuscript in his handwriting, apparently the end of some queer narrative, which Mrs Maberley had torn from the hand of the departing felon.

The next thing I knew, we were back on the train and then speeding in a cab to some address in Grosvenor Square. And there – to my enormous astonishment – he confronted the very person who, he reasoned, was ultimately responsible for the burglary, and indeed the whole mystery. We left without committing anyone into the hands of the law – but with a cheque large enough to send Mrs Maberley round the world in first-class style.

A short railway journey, and a shorter drive, had taken us to the brick and timber house with the three gables. During the journey, my friend ventured another of his little puzzles for me to solve.

'Look at these words, Watson. Which English word can be attached to the end of all the words to the left, and to the beginning of all the words on the right, such that it makes six new words?' And he drew the puzzle out for me as follows:

$$
\left.\begin{array}{l} \textbf{COPY} \\ \textbf{SCRAP} \\ \textbf{HAND} \end{array}\right\} \quad \textbf{- - - -} \quad \left\{\begin{array}{l} \textbf{WORM} \\ \textbf{CASES} \\ \textbf{MARK} \end{array}\right.
$$

65. The Sussex Vampire

'It has been a case for intellectual deduction, but when this original intellectual deduction is confirmed point by point by quite a number of independent incidents, then the subjective becomes objective and we can say confidently that we have reached our goal. I had, in fact, reached it before we left Baker Street, and the rest has merely been observation and confirmation.'

THE EXTRAORDINARY suggestion that some horror from darkest Transylvania had now come to haunt the residents of quietest Surrey came to us one November in a letter from an old rugby acquaintance of mine, Robert Ferguson.

The case concerned the daughter of a Peruvian merchant, recently married to Ferguson, a widower living in Lamberley, near Horsham. Not only had she assaulted her fifteen-year-old stepson in an unprovoked way; but then she was seen bending over her own infant, apparently biting his neck. The husband could not believe this bizarre news – until he himself found the woman rising from the infant's cot, and saw blood on the child's neck and all around her lips.

Next day we took the two o'clock train from Victoria and deposited our bags at the Chequers in Lamberley before driving to Ferguson's isolated and ancient farmhouse. He introduced us to his household, including his rather lame and decrepit spaniel, which Holmes apparently thought to be a significant part of this strange story, though I could not see why.

It took Holmes no time to confirm his suspicions and

unravel the truth from these bizarre events. The explanation would bring much joy, but almost equal sadness, to the Ferguson household.

As we took lunch before setting out to Victoria on our way down to Lamberley, Holmes outlined another of his little puzzles – which he probably intended to keep me occupied while he pondered the case on the train.

'Fine repast you are enjoying there, Watson. Puts me quite in the mood to test your reflexes.' And he scribbled out an array of letters on the back of the hotel-bill. 'Tell me,' he went on, 'starting with the word LUNCH, how can you complete this square so that four more English words can be read downwards and across, using only the letters A, A, D, E, E, E, F, L, L, S, S, T, T, U, U and V?'

He tossed the paper over to me. 'I very much doubt that someone of your intellectual abilities should need more than ten minutes for such a trivial little problem – unless, perhaps, that substantial feast has dulled your brain.'

So I set to work on the puzzle he had drawn out thus:

L U N C H
U
N
C
H

66. The Three Garridebs

'You are, of course, the Mr John Garrideb mentioned in this
document. But surely you have been in England some time?'
'Why do you say that, Mr Holmes?' I seemed to read
sudden suspicion in those expressive eyes.
'Your whole outfit is English.'
Mr Garrideb forced a laugh. 'I've read of your tricks, Mr
Holmes, but I never thought I would be the subject of them.
Where do you read that?'
'The shoulder cut of your coat, the toes of your boots –
could anyone doubt it?'

IT WAS A CASE, as I have said in my account of it, that
may have been a comedy or a tragedy. It cost one man
his reason, me a blood-letting, and another man the
penalties of the law. And yet there were comic elements
to it.

I remember the date, June 1902, because Holmes had
just refused a knighthood. A letter had come from a Mr
Nathan Garrideb. I was pondering this unusual name when
another Garrideb – a Mr John Garrideb of Kansas, USA –
strode into the room.

He told us how the late Alexander Hamilton Garrideb,
a wealthy Chicago trader with no known relatives, had left
him a one-third share of his fifteen-million-dollar estate –
provided that he could find two other Garridebs to share
the remainder.

It was a remarkable story, which Holmes instantly
perceived as a tissue of lies. So we called upon Mr Nathan
Garrideb in his ground-floor apartment in Little Ryder
Street, one of the smaller offshoots from the Edgware

Road. He was a gaunt, eccentric character, and his room looked like a small museum, crowded with geological and anatomical specimens of every kind.

This Mr Garrideb – and Holmes instantly deduced that Garrideb *was* the real name of this gentleman, at least – was something of a recluse who never left his small home and the astonishing collection it contained.

Just then our American visitor burst in, clutching a Birmingham paper that bore an advertisement for the services of one Howard Garrideb, a constructor of agricultural machinery in Aston. It seemed to me that our client, and the American, would get their share of the fortune after all. It was resolved that, though it was certainly not his normal habit to venture out, Mr Nathan Garrideb would take tomorrow's mid-day train to the Midlands to see the third Garrideb and in person extract an affidavit of his existence that would satisfy the American lawyers.

Holmes had made arrangements to re-visit Little Ryder Street when he was out on his travels, and Mr Nathan Garrideb – delighted that another intelligent man should take an interest in his collection – made arrangements with the housekeeper to admit him. And so it was that at four o'clock the next day we found ourselves back in the empty apartment.

But Holmes's true motive was not to inspect the strange specimens; rather, it was to find the solution to this extraordinary case. It was a visit which left me with a leg wound – though in my friend's concern for me, I caught my one and only glimpse of the great heart which co-existed with his great brain.

Anyway, following the first appearance of our American acquaintance, we had arranged to call upon Mr Nathan Garrideb at six o'clock. That gave us a few hours to while away. So my friend suggested a little diversion.

*'I will be at your service in one instant, Watson. You will find
the tobacco in the Persian slipper.'*

'The advertisement for agricultural machinery set me
thinking,' said he. 'Which English word can be attached
to the end of the words in the left-hand column, and to
the beginning of the words in the right-hand column to
form six new words?'

I looked over the words he had written down:

$$\left.\begin{array}{l} \textbf{GRIST} \\ \textbf{WIND} \\ \textbf{SAW} \end{array}\right\} \; - - - - \; \left\{\begin{array}{l} \textbf{POND} \\ \textbf{WHEEL} \\ \textbf{ION} \end{array}\right.$$

'Oh, dear, Holmes,' said I – for I had come across his little word-games often before, and knew that hidden traps often lurked for the unwary – 'how long do I have this time?'

'Well, Watson,' he replied, 'someone in the top 3% of the intelligence range should, I reckon, be able to solve that little amusement in no more than eight minutes.'

Nervously I set to work.

67. The Problem of Thor Bridge

'Let me say right here, Mr Holmes,' he began, 'that money is nothing to me in this case. You can burn it if it's any use in lighting you to the truth. This woman is innocent and this woman has to be cleared, and it's up to you to do it. Name your figure!'

'My professional charges are upon a fixed scale,' said Holmes coldly. 'I do not vary them, save when I remit them altogether.'

I T WAS A wild morning in early October, and Holmes's bright and cheerful manner indicated to me that he had a new case to occupy him. It had come in a letter from

J. Neil Gibson, former US Senator for a Western state, and the greatest gold-mining magnate in the world.

Holmes was already familiar with the facts of the case. Gibson's wife was discovered dead in the grounds of their grand old manor house, a revolver bullet through her brain. No weapon had been found near her. Suspicion fell upon Miss Grace Dunbar, the attractive governess to the two young children: on the floor of her wardrobe was discovered a revolver with one discharged chamber and a calibre matching that of the fatal bullet.

Even before the Gold King had called upon us in person, Holmes had deduced that his relationship with Miss Dunbar was more than merely professional. Had Mrs Gibson discovered this affair and been killed in a dispute about it? Then there was a note in Miss Dunbar's hand, saying that she would be at Thor Bridge at nine o'clock – the scene and the time of the incident. Things certainly looked black against the governess.

We went down to Winchester, and visited the accused in her cell. She confirmed that Mrs Gibson hated her and was racked with jealousy. It was not a long journey from there to Thor Place, but both of us were impatient, particularly my friend. In his usual curt manner he tossed out a problem to occupy me and so to avoid distraction, while he himself fidgeted nervously, wishing the journey were over so that he could be back on the chase again.

'Listen carefully, Watson, I shall say this just once. Attach the same letter – the same letter, mark you – to each of the following groups of letters, and then rearrange them to form four English words. You will find that the missing letter will occur at the centre of each word you have formed.

'Now,' he said, handing over a fragment of paper –

bearing the letters ABEH, CDHI, AELR and AELM –
'tell me when you have found the missing letter, but in
the meantime, pray grant me a little silence so I might
think.'

68. The Creeping Man

*'You will excuse a certain abstraction of mind, my dear
Watson,' said he. 'Some curious facts have been submitted to
me within the last twenty-four hours, and they in turn have
given rise to some speculations of a more general character. I
have serious thoughts of writing a small monograph upon the
uses of dogs in the work of the detective.'*
'But surely, Holmes, this has been explored,' said I.
'Bloodhounds – sleuth-hounds – '
*'No, no, Watson, that side of the matter is, of course,
obvious. But there is another which is far more subtle . . . A
dog reflects the family life. Whoever saw a frisky dog in a
gloomy family, or a sad dog in a happy one? Snarling people
have snarling dogs, dangerous people have dangerous ones.
And their passing moods may reflect the passing moods of
others.'*

'**W**HY DOES PROFESSOR Presbury's wolfhound, Roy,
endeavour to bite him?' That was the – apparently
rather disappointing – question for which I had rushed to
Baker Street on Holmes's laconic summons in that September of 1903.

But in fact the question proved to be the key to a much
deeper and more sinister mystery than I had supposed.

Indeed, the Professor, a man of European reputation, was bitten only on certain occasions. Nor did the dog attack anyone else.

It had all started when the Professor, at the age of sixty-one, had become engaged to the daughter of a colleague. Next he was off on a trip to Prague, but then his character changed to being furtive and sly. On July 2nd, 11th and 20th he was inexplicably attacked by his dog. After another attack on August the 26th, the poor animal, normally a most affectionate creature, was banished to the stables.

Then, on the night of September the 4th, the Professor was seen coming along the dark passage of his house – but crawling! And his daughter too was astonished and frightened to see his face outside the window of her second-floor bedroom!

There would be further curious and tragic incidents before Holmes had revealed their cause. We set off to meet the Professor and have a look at the scene of his extraordinary climb to the second floor. As we relaxed in the sitting-room of the ancient hotel, my friend announced that no further developments could be expected until the following Tuesday, so we had time to enjoy the amenities of that charming town.

We also had time to spend in some idle amusement, and it was not long before Holmes was setting me another infuriating puzzle.

'Well, Watson, we have ten minutes, so tell me this. Which English word, when attached to the front of GO, COURT, WARN, THOUGHT, and LEG, will create five other English words?'

69. The Lion's Mane

The inspector remained, staring at me in silence with his ox-like eyes.
'Well, you've done it!' he cried at last. 'I had read of you, but I never believed it. It's wonderful.'
I was forced to shake my head. To accept such praise was to lower one's own standards.
– Sherlock Holmes

IN JULY 1907, my friend Mr Sherlock Holmes was enjoying the air near his retirement villa on the south coast when a most abstruse and unusual event occurred before his eyes. As he has described in *The Adventure of the Lion's Mane*, there on the clifftop he saw Fitzroy McPherson, the local science master, stagger like a drunken man and fall on to his face.

Only the words 'the Lion's Mane' slurred from his lips before he shuddered and fell dead.

It was a most suspicious death. The deceased had an intimate correspondence with Miss Maud Bellamy, who had arranged to meet him at the beach and accordingly fell under suspicion. So did her father and brother, who opposed the friendship. So too did Ian Murdoch, the mathematics coach, a man of occasionally ferocious temper, who had argued with McPherson.

But the incident that pointed my friend to a solution of the case was the subsequent death of McPherson's dog, presumed to have expired from grief for its master, at the very same spot along the shore. And the appearance of Ian Murdoch, showing exactly the same symptoms as those of

the unfortunate victim, led Holmes directly to the solution
– and the extraordinary killer.

Reading through Holmes's account reminded me of one
time I had visited him in his retirement. He was conducting
me through his impressive collection of bees, to which he
had now devoted his whole energies, when he put to me
the following riddle.

'This seems an appropriate little rhyme for you,' he
remarked, and so I will give you only five minutes to solve
it.'

> 'My first is in CHIME but not in BELL,
> 'My next is in SHORE but not in SHELL,
> 'My third is in SONG and also in TUNE,
> 'My fourth is in PLANET but not in MOON,
> 'My fifth is in DINGHY and also in YACHT,
> 'My whole it is sticky and found in a pot;
> 'What am I?'

70. The Veiled Lodger

*The discretion and high sense of professional honour which
have always distinguished my friend are still at work in the
choice of these memoirs, and no confidence will be abused. I
deprecate, however, in the strongest way the attempts which
have been made lately to get at and to destroy these papers.
The source of these outrages is known, and if they are repeated
I have Mr Holmes's authority for saying that the whole story
concerning the politician, the lighthouse, and the trained*

cormorant will be given to the public. There is at least one
reader who will understand.

ONE FORENOON late in 1896 I was summoned by a hurried note from Holmes. When I arrived, he introduced me to a Mrs Merrilow, of South Brixton, who was in the middle of an account concerning her lodger, Mrs Ronder.

It seemed that Mrs Ronder suffered the misfortune of having a disfigured face, which she kept permanently veiled. But matters were brought to a head by a decline in her health due to some deep trouble of the soul. She would cry out 'Murder!' and 'You cruel beast!' as if there was something terrible on her mind.

Holmes and I arranged to call and meet this mysterious lodger; but no sooner had Mrs Merrilow waddled out of the room than Holmes immediately descended on his prodigious files and in a few minutes had identified Mrs Ronder to me as one of the unfortunate victims of the Abbas Parva tragedy – 'The case worried me at the time, Watson.'

As our hansom made its way through the West End and over the bridge towards South Brixton that afternoon, Holmes explained more of the background of the case to me, and the chain of thought led him on to a less serious question.

'The lady acquired her unfortunate disfigurement,' he recounted, 'by being mauled by a circus lion – or at least, that is how it was reported at the time. It brings to mind another little enigma that seems appropriate to these circumstances. Let me outline it for you.

'One day, on a trip to the circus menagerie, Luke visited the elephants, saw the kangaroos and fed the llama, which came from Uruguay. So who do you think it was, Watson, who laughed at the apes from Kenya, saw the monkeys and helped bath the rhinoceros?'

I had to admit that I had absolutely no idea.

71. Shoscombe Old Place

'It is glue, Watson,' said he. 'Unquestionably it is glue. Have a look at these scattered objects in the field.'

I stooped to the eyepiece and focused for my vision.

'Those hairs are threads from a tweed coat. The irregular gray masses are dust. There are epithelial scales on the left. Those brown blobs in the centre are undoubtedly glue.'

'Well,' I said, laughing. 'I am prepared to take your word for it. Does anything depend upon it?'

'It is a very fine demonstration,' he answered. 'In the St Pancras case you may remember that a cap was found beside the dead policeman. The accused man denies that it is his. But he is a picture-frame maker who habitually handles glue.'

'Is it one of your cases?'

'No; my friend, Merivale, of the Yard, asked me to look into the case. Since I ran down that coiner by the zinc and copper filings in the seam of his cuff they have begun to realize the importance of the microscope.'

SINCE ABOUT half of my wound pension goes to subsidize the British racing industry, I was able to give my companion quite a few details about the mercurial owner Sir Robert Norberton and his training establishment at Shoscombe Park.

But the story told to us by Sir Robert's head trainer, John Mason, contained details far more queer than any I had heard about the tempestuous baronet. There was the point about how his sister Lady Beatrice had suddenly lost interest in her stables; that she had suddenly taken to drinking heavily; of the master's nocturnal visits to the old church crypt to meet some unknown person; how he had given away her favourite dog; and of the charred fragment of bone found in the household furnace.

Plainly, something had cut deep into the life of the Shoscombe establishment. Holmes volunteered us to go down that bright May evening, staying at the Green Dragon and ostensibly on a fishing expedition to see if we could entice any of the local pike and trout to rise to our bait.

After some enquiries the next morning my companion seemed to have no further plans, and we did in fact get the chance to use our fishing tackle in the mill-stream. The result was not only a dish of trout for supper, but some cheerful and relaxed conversation on various subjects.

One element of the conversation, I recall, was the following characteristic query from Holmes.

'A horseman – let us call him Sir Robert – rides from one town to another,' he said. 'On the first day he covers one-half of the total distance. The next day he covers a quarter of what is left. The following day he covers half of the remainder, and on the fourth day one-quarter of the remaining difference.'

By this time, I was scribbling furiously on my shirt-cuff.

'Now,' continued my friend, 'at the end of all that, our horseman has eleven and one-quarter miles left. Got that? Good! So now tell me: How far has he travelled? And don't take all day, Watson – ten minutes should be quite sufficient.' And he cast his line out once again.

158

72. The Retired Colourman

'I saw him once more at London Bridge, and then I lost him in the crowd. But I am convinced that he was following me.'
'No doubt! No doubt!' said Holmes. 'A tall, dark, heavily moustached man, you say, with gray-tinted sun-glasses?'
'Holmes, you are a wizard. I did not say so, but he had gray-tinted sun-glasses.'
'And a Masonic tie-pin?'
'Holmes!'
'Quite simple, my dear Watson.'

HOLMES BEING preoccupied with the case of the two Coptic Patriarchs, he sent me off to collect information that might give us some insight into the whereabouts of Dr Ray Ernest and the wife of Josiah Amberley, the retired manufacturer of artistic materials, who had gone off together – destination unknown – taking the old colourman's deed-box with them.

I was rather crestfallen when, on my return, Holmes chided me for missing everything of importance about the case, and for being quite unaware of the major significance of the details which I had indeed collected.

My colleague made an early start the next morning; and returned that afternoon to say that he expected Josiah Amberley quite soon. The old man followed shortly, bearing a mysterious telegram dispatched from the vicar of Little Purlington, in Essex. Holmes opined that it was a clue worth pursuing, and so Amberley and I were dispatched on the 5.20 from Liverpool Street.

My travelling companion had the reputation of being a miser and a misanthrope, and the journey convinced me that both were correct. He hardly ventured a remark on the journey down; he was scornful when we discovered that our errand had been a wild goose chase; and on the way back he was even more unpleasant.

At first I tried to reassure him about the value and success of Holmes's methods, and cited a few similar cases in which he had been triumphant, like the case of the Grice Patersons in Uffa, and the affair he investigated for Mr Fairdale Hobbs. But since my travelling companion would not listen to such talk, I thought I might see if I could divert him with a little puzzle, and amuse him out of his desolate shell. I pondered hard to devise something appropriate, and then put it to him.

'We seem to be in the middle of nowhere,' I remarked. Amberley raised a single eyebrow, but otherwise appeared unmoved. 'If Swindon is 45 miles away,' I continued, 'Gloucester is 62 miles away and Cheltenham is 64 miles away, then how far away are we from Worcester?'

The miser, however, was still in no mood for civilities and gave a contemptuous grunt.

UNCOLLECTED CASES OF SHERLOCK HOLMES

73. The Tall Man

*There is a disused well, which has not been searched because
apparently nothing is missing. Sherlock, however, insists on the
well being explored. A village boy consents to be lowered into
it, with a candle. Before he goes down, Holmes whispers
something in his ear – he appears surprised. The boy is lowered
and, on his signal, pulled up again. He brings to the surface a
pair of stilts!*

*'Good Lord!' cries the detective, 'who on earth could have
expected this?'*

'I did,' replies Holmes.

I REMEMBER A particularly curious case in which Holmes
was able to clear the name of a man arrested for murder
despite the most damning evidence. The suspect had a
violent quarrel with the victim that previous evening; a
revolver was found in his house; and marks in the soil

beneath the victim's bedroom exactly matched the foot of the ladder which he possessed.

Unfortunately I never had time to write a complete narrative based on this case, though I am sure that it would have been of some interest to my readers. Perhaps, if these papers which I am depositing in a tin box with Cox & Co excite the interest of some future writer, it may yet appear.*

Anyway, in response to a plea from the suspect's charming lover, Holmes and I, together with the detective in charge of the case, found ourselves driving towards the scene of the crime. Holmes could never resist the temptation to tease any official detective whenever he had an idle moment to devote to such a diversion; and so it was not long before another of his little conundrums was produced with the aim of bewildering the inspector.

'Inspector,' said my friend, 'I will give you six minutes only for you to prove your ability to answer this question. Consider the words ANT, BOY, HOOD, BEEF, WINK, BULLY, EATER and FOND. Now, these eight words will form four larger words when each is matched with its correct pair. Pray tell me what those larger words happen to be.'

* *Editors' note:* It would seem that Watson did not seal up the only copy of this synopsis, but kept another, perhaps intending to write up the story himself later if he ever found time. This latter version came into the hands of an American enthusiast, Robert A. Cutter, who in 1947 wrote the full story around the outline. It is one of the items collected by Peter Haining in *The Final Adventures of Sherlock Holmes* (Warner Books, 1981).

74. The Man Who Was Wanted

Holmes was stretched upon the couch with his back towards me, the familiar dressing-gown and old brier pipe as much in evidence as of yore.

'Come in, Watson,' he cried, without glancing round. 'Come in and tell me what good wind blows you here?'

'What an ear you have, Holmes,' I said. 'I don't think that I could have recognized your tread so easily.'

'Nor I yours,' said he, 'if you hadn't come up my badly lighted staircase taking the steps two at a time with all the familiarity of an old fellow lodger; even then I might not have been sure who it was, but when you stumbled over the new mat outside the door which has been there for nearly three months, you needed no further announcement.'

I DID NOT include this case among my other recollections of the remarkable talents of Mr Sherlock Holmes. Though it was a singular and astonishing illustration of my friend's powers of deduction, I felt that my account of it was of insufficient quality to maintain the interest of the discerning reader.

The case involved a remarkable fraud effected in Sheffield by Mr Jabez Booth, a former employee of the British Consolidated Bank, who had now made his escape and disappeared. As we called at the house where Mr Booth had been a lodger for more than seven years, we found Mr Lestrade of Scotland Yard, who was delighted to inform us that he had discovered the man's escape plans and would effect an arrest soon.

'There's our man, Watson! Come along.'

The evidence in question was the impression, left on an old blotter, of a letter in Booth's handwriting, and directed to a booking agency in Liverpool, reserving a first-class private cabin and passage on board the *Empress Queen* to New York.

Holmes, however, retained an enigmatical silence on the matter of this apparently sensational clue. He preferred to employ his own methods, and to make his own enquiries; so while he busied himself around Sheffield, he dispatched me to the art gallery and museum with an injunction that I should find some more entertaining way of spending the rest of the day.

I passed a few hours in the gallery, where I suddenly discovered in my coat pocket one of the little conundrums that Holmes occasionally wrote for his own amusement, and which he had obviously secreted on me in the hope that I might find it as I searched around for amusement that day. It read as follows.

Watson – local canals interesting. Saw one barge on its way to another town, noted progress as follows:

First day: barge covered one-fifth of the total distance. Second day: covered another fifth of what was left. Third day: covered one-third of the remainder. Fourth day: travelled one-half of the remaining distance.

Barge now had twenty-six and two-thirds miles still to travel. How far had it come already?

[signed] Holmes

PS: Ten minutes only!

ANSWERS AND EXPLANATIONS

A Study in Scarlet

1. Mr Sherlock Holmes

The wine cost 5 pence. The cider, at half the cost, was 2 and one-half pence. The four bottles of cider were thus 10 pence, and the wine made it 15 pence between the two of us, or sevenpence ha'penny each.

'Pshaw!' said Mr Sherlock Holmes as, some time later, I outlined the mental difficulties which this calculation had given us. 'Anyone in the top 7% of the intelligence range, with an IQ of 134 or more, should have been able to answer that in a twinkling!'

2. The Lauriston Gardens Mystery

At first I ventured a guess at 112 hours, which my colleague pronounced as wrong. When my time was up, he gave me the correct answer, which was 114 hours.

'The 98 candles give 1 hour each,' he explained. 'The

98 stubs make a further 14 candles giving 14 hours, and the 14 stubs from them make a further 2 candles. Total, 114.'

3. Light in the Darkness

'The type of French priest is an Abbé,' Holmes explained. 'You see, the word RACHE can be made square by reducing it to numbers. If A = 1, B = 2, etc., the word becomes 18 + 1 + 3 + 8 + 5, which equals 35. The square of 35 is 1225. The letters corresponding to these numbers are ABBE, which is . . .'

'A type of priest. By Jove, Holmes! I thought this was a very complicated problem, but now you have explained it to me I see that the solution is simplicity itself.'

Holmes gave me a withering look.

4. The Flower of Utah

The unnamed city turned out to be 1,600 miles from London.

'The fact that you required no Atlas should have been a clue, Watson,' commented my friend. 'It is the names, and not the actual locations, which are important.'

And he explained: 'In the names of each of the cities referred to, the vowels count for 200 miles each, the consonants for 300 miles each. London is thus 2 × 200 + 4 × 300 miles away. Really, Watson! It doesn't take an IQ of more than 148 to work that out! Top 2% should be able to do that easily! Finished with the *Echo?*'

The Sign of Four

5. The Science of Deduction

The connection I found is that all the words have the name of a container within them, namely POT, CUP, PAN, EWER and TIN. According to Mr Sherlock Holmes, my successful solution of this problem within the five minutes he gave me suggested that I had an IQ rating of around 143 – among the top 3% of the population.

6. The Tragedy of Pondicherry Lodge

The words I found were SHORE, SHARE, SHALE, SHALL and SMALL, but Holmes told me there might be other ways of doing it. Once again, the verdict was that my IQ was at or over the 143 figure.

7. Sherlock Holmes Gives a Demonstration

The answer, Holmes told me, was 4 years.

'Do not be disappointed that you got this one wrong, my friend,' said he, soothingly. 'One has to be exceptionally clever to answer such a problem correctly, even within the generous time that was at hand.'

'You mean, as bright as one person in a thousand?'

'Well,' he replied, 'as bright as one in a hundred – an IQ rating of 161 or thereabouts.'

8. The End of the Islander

I wished that I had spent more of my youth in the study of geography. The four island chains in question were Aleutian, Scilly, Azores and Maldives. The letters Holmes indicated can be rearranged to spell CAYMAN, which is the answer.

'Can't even claim to be in the top 2%, Watson? IQ rating less than 148? Hum!'

The Adventures of Sherlock Holmes

9. A Scandal in Bohemia

'What on earth are all these doodles, Watson?' asked my friend when he had shuffled off his disguise, returned to his familiar identity, and told me the astonishing events of the day.

'I was just trying to work out this question about the connection between these different words,' I replied. 'But I confess that I am still quite bamboozled.'

'My dear Watson, it's elementary. And quite appropriate, given the musical nature of our quarry in this case. Unscramble the letters and you get the names of four musical instruments: ORGAN, CLARINET, TROMBONE, and XYLOPHONE.'

10. The Red-headed League

'Something on your mind, I perceive, Watson,' said my friend as we moved to set our trap for the intending criminal that night.

'Well, er . . .'

'Undoubtedly that scrap of paper I saw you pocket is still puzzling you. The words are mixed up, my friend: they are the names of three household items, namely CONTAINER, CORKSCREW and CAKESTAND. Now be quiet, if you please, and let us be about our business.'

11. A Case of Identity

'Your time is about to expire and I would not wish to leave you thinking I had such a low opinion of you,' said my friend at last. 'So let me tell you now before the deadline comes. Some 33 pints were drunk in all, Watson. Charlie drank 12, Spike drank 2, Tom drank 9, Mick drank 4 and Brian drank 6. It was, as you can imagine, quite a jolly evening!'

12. The Boscombe Valley Mystery

'Nutmeg, cinnamon, ginger and coriander,' I said at last, as we ventured on to the platform to see our connecting train draw in.

'Excellent, Watson!' cried my friend. 'That shows you have an IQ of 148 or more – the top 2% of the population!'

13. The Five Orange Pips

Eventually I worked out the answer. Holmes was quite right, only five steps were needed: BOON, BOOR, BOAR, SOAR and STAR.

14. The Man with the Twisted Lip

The answer turned out to be 17 minutes and 19 seconds, to the nearest second. Holmes told me that anyone solving this problem in the eight minutes I was given must have had an IQ of 140 or more, putting them in the top 4% for intelligence.

15. The Blue Carbuncle

It turned out that the letter S would have to appear in the bottom left-hand position.

16. The Speckled Band

Holmes told me later that anyone solving this puzzle in the ten minutes which I had could be adjudged to have an IQ of 150 or more, putting them easily into the top 2% of the population. The missing word was, almost appropriately, ANACONDA, making the compounds TARTAN and ANTHEM, SHELLAC and ACCLAIM, CARTON and ONRUSH, and PANDA and DARED.

17. The Engineer's Thumb

Our engineer friend knew his business well. He had the answer – 144 revolutions – almost before I had even jotted the numbers down on a piece of paper.

18. The Noble Bachelor

Holmes calculated in an instant what it had taken me an evening to work out: Miss Doran ought to have received a cheque for $2.85.

19. The Beryl Coronet

'Ha! Ha! Dr Watson!' said our acquaintance nervously when he saw how much I was struggling. 'It took me a while to work it out too, until I realized that the single letters must be placed along the diagonals, and the pairs placed either side. The words are NIGH, OGRE, and WHEY. But lo! I see we are almost at our destination!'

20. The Copper Beeches

The middle letter of each word can be used to form the seasonal word SPRING.

The Memoirs of Sherlock Holmes

21. Silver Blaze

There were 336 potatoes. Holmes explained that each vowel in the names of the various fireworks is worth 3 and each consonant is worth 7. When the totals in each word are multiplied, it produces exactly the number that the quartermaster provided.

'A clear enough pattern Watson,' he continued. 'So when you confirmed that Higgins had also prepared some potatoes, it was a simple matter to perform the same calculation on the name of that vegetable and thus to deduce precisely how many were consumed.'

And he explained that if you solved this in the specified twelve minutes you could reasonably claim to have an IQ rating of 148 – within the top 2% of the population!

22. The Yellow Face

After re-checking my figures a few times I concluded that 56 people lived in the village. Holmes confirmed this as correct.

23. The Stock-broker's Clerk

Holmes explained later that the answer was 6 and 5. It turned out that the first figure in each row, multiplied by the third, equalled the fifth; while the second figure and the fourth figure summed to produce the sixth figure on each row.

24. The 'Gloria Scott'

When I asked Holmes about this strange figure, he told me that the answer was 33, explaining that the alphabetical values of the two letters on each line (A = 1, B = 2, etc.) are added to give the figure in the centre.

25. The Musgrave Ritual

The answer did indeed remind one of the grounds of the Manor House, with its famous collection of formidable and ancient trees. Holmes's words all contained the name of a different tree, namely: ASH, ELM, OAK and FIR.

26. The Reigate Squire

I had the answer within the ten minutes allotted, which Holmes pointed out put me in the top 3% of the population, with an IQ rating of 143 or above.

The number of copies for each volume are the sum of the roman numerals in the title. Thus M = 1000, D = 500, C = 100, L = 50, × = 10 (though there are none in these examples) and I = 1. So the figure for NICHOLAS NICKLEBY turned out to be 302 copies.

27. The Crooked Man

Holmes confirmed that, yes, the engine would be able to put out the fire; and he showed me the relevant calculations. One divides the distance to the destination by the speed of the engine in order to find the time the journey will take – in this case 0.2931 hours. If the engine leaks 10 gallons per hour, it will therefore lose 2.931 gallons in that time, leaving it only just a little more than the 147 gallons required.

28. The Resident Patient

The answer was BRAIN – which I suppose any medical man ought to have detected – making BARGE and BEAST, REACH and RATIO, ACORN and APACE, IRATE and IRONY, NASTY and NAILS.

29. The Greek Interpreter

The answer was two and one-third years – though I had to wait until Mr Mycroft Holmes could explain it to me, and even then I could not fully understand the argument until I returned to my lodging and mapped out the whole solar system on a sheet of paper.

30. The Naval Treaty

The answer was TRICK. One has to take the appropriate letters to spell the word.

31. The Final Problem

The answer was 9. Holmes explained that the right-hand number, minus the left-hand number, gives the centre number. In other words $75 - 69 = 6$, $19 - 11 = 8$, and $57 - 48 = 9$.

'It serves to show very clearly how simple the explanation may be of an affair which at first sight seems almost inexplicable,' commented my friend.

The Hound of the Baskervilles

32. The Curse of the Baskervilles

The chosen letters have to be C&H, E&S, T&N and U&T. Of course, together they spell CHESTNUT, which I had to agree is indeed something best eaten hot.

33. Sir Henry Baskerville

'Really, Holmes, this question must be impossible to answer!' I remonstrated. 'There must be thousands of them. Possibly even millions.'

'Ah, Watson! My one fixed point in a changing universe! No, there are in fact *no* nine-digit prime numbers which use all nine digits, no matter what the order.'

As Holmes explained it, the numbers 1,2,3,4,5,6,7,8,9 add up to a number (45) that is divisible by 3. It is a commonplace rule that any number showing this feature is itself divisible by 3; the arrangement of digits does not matter. 'So since every allowable number, from 123,456,789 to 987,654,321 is divisible by 3, none of them can be prime.'

34. Baskerville Hall

The letters Holmes wanted were T and E. When TE is inserted in WARS, PANT, EARS and LAST, it makes the four words WATERS, PATENT, EATERS and LATEST. Although it is I who write about his adventures, I have to confess that he is infinitely more clever with words as playthings.

35. Death on the Moor

Holmes's solution to this question actually caused us to argue. I had first worked out that 12 was one such number, since 12 squared is 144, and 21 squared is 441. I also had 11, because 11 squared is 121, whose reverse is the square of the reverse of 11.

'Sorry, Watson,' he interjected, 'you cannot have that one because we said no palindromes, and 11 reads the same backwards as well as forwards.'

Holmes then supplied 13, whose square is 169, the reverse of which gives 961, the square of 31. I was happy to accept this and was disappointed that I had not had enough time to work that far through the numerical series.

I was outraged by Holmes's third number, however. He

added the figure 10, because its square – 100 – when reversed, gives 001. 'And that, as you will readily perceive,' he said smugly, 'is the square of 10's reverse – 01!'

I called it trickery, but Holmes insisted the answers were 10, 12 and 13. I still wanted my 11 to count, but Holmes said that if palindromes were allowed we would have to include 22, 33, 101, 111, 121, 222, 232, 1001, 1111, and 20002 . . .

I stopped him there and did not press the point.

The Return of Sherlock Holmes

36. The Empty House

I was just able to provide the correct answer in time. 'It must have been 23,' I said, proudly. (I had calculated that on the first 30 shots he must have scored a total of 450, on the first 40 shots he had amassed a total of 680; so on the last 10 he had collected 680 – 450 (= 230) points, an average of 23 per shot.)

'Quite right, Watson, and a very remarkable score it was. That is why I have always kept a close eye on the whereabouts and activities of Colonel Sebastian Moran, whom I anticipate we will meet tonight. So keep your wits sharp, my friend! The game's afoot!'

37. The Norwood Builder

Since I was not under any time pressure I eventually worked out, to my satisfaction at least, that there were five ways of collecting the necessary letters.

38. The Dancing Men

I was being teased. The hidden quotation read: ADVICE TO PERSONS ABOUT TO MARRY – DON'T!

39. The Solitary Cyclist

At first I thought the answer must be 12 and one-half miles per hour, but eventually my companion convinced me that the answer was 8 m.p.h. To visualise the answer, it is easiest to work in miles. Suppose the hill is absurdly large, 20 miles up and 20 miles down. Then at 5 m.p.h. the first leg would take 4 hours while the downhill journey at 20 m.p.h. would take only 1 hour. Thus the total journey of 40 miles would take 5 hours – an average speed of 40/5 or 8 m.p.h. But the average speed would be the same whether each half of the journey was 20 yards, 20 feet, or 20 anythings.

40. The Priory School

'Ho, ho, ho! Dr Watson! You are teasing me,' said our client at last. 'Why, the answer is MASTER. Its letters make up the pairs DOGMA and MASON, TRYST and

STAID, and CAPER and ERRED. But I must say that I found TRYST a little hard to grasp at first.'

41. Black Peter

Unfortunately, as I explained to the inspector, the ship would *not* in fact achieve its target. We fared rather better on our own little excursion that evening. Against the 1 knot tide, the ship can make 7 knots (that is, 8−1), and so will reach its harbour, 25 miles away, in 25/7 hours. Using 12 hundred weight of coal each hour, the whole trip will therefore consume 12 × (25/7) hundred weight, which mental arithmetic shows to be 42.857 hundred weight. Unfortunately the ship is carrying slightly less, so will not in fact reach its harbour.

42. Charles Augustus Milverton

Holmes told me later that the vile swindler had sold 140 letters, at 215 guineas each. 'No other combination of number and price – within the range I specified – would give you the fabulous sum of 3010 guineas, Watson. But let us turn our minds to less repulsive subjects than the odious activities of the late Charles Augustus Milverton!'

43. The Six Napoleons

It was sound advice indeed for a peppery shopkeeper. When you ignore the spacings and read the string of letters backwards, you will find it reads: THE CUSTOMER IS ALWAYS RIGHT.

44. The Three Students

I knew a little about cricket from my college days, but I did not have to understand the game – only some elementary mathematics – to perceive that the average number of runs scored over the last 4 innings must have been 34.

45. The Golden Pince-nez

The odd combination of letters was BRTT. With the appropriate vowels interspersed, it gives BEETROOT. The others are TULIP, DAFFODIL and CROCUS.

'Oh, I see, Holmes! The odd one out is a vegetable, while the others are all flowers!'

'No, my dear fellow,' he replied. 'The others flourish in the spring, while a beetroot is unusable until the end of the summer.'

I was not exactly certain whether or not I was being teased by The Great Detective.

46. The Missing Three-quarter

'I still beat him, Watson, despite the fact that he thought he was going to win by a yard. Do you think I had not calculated it? I'm glad that, after it was all over, Warburton too could see the funny side of my little ruse.'

Holmes explained that while he had run 400 yards in the relevant time – let us say, one minute – his opponent had covered only 380 yards in that period. In the second race, Holmes had to cover 421 yards, which he did at his established speed of 400 yards per minute. This took him

421/400 = 1.0525 minutes. His opponent had only 400 yards to cover, but at his established speed of 380 yards per minute, this (Holmes knew) would take him slightly longer, at 1.0526 minutes. So Holmes proved himself more agile mentally as well as physically.

47. The Abbey Grange

The answer turned out to be 33.

I remained puzzled, until Holmes told me that there were two series of numbers, interspersed alternately. In one – 5, 10, 15, 20, 25 – the numbers rise by 5 each time. In the other – 3, 5, 9, 17, 33 – the numbers rise by steps of 2, 4, 8, and (of course) 16.

48. The Second Stain

Holmes explained that the next destination was Canada. He had detected the following pattern: the first letter of the first country visited gives the first letter of the spy's name; the second letter of the second country visited gives the second letter of the name; the third letter of the third country gives the third letter of the name; and so on.

So of the countries I randomly suggested, only Canada would fit the pattern. Holmes said that anyone solving this problem in fifteen minutes could reasonably claim to be in the top 1% of the population, with an IQ of 155 or more.

'It is quite a three-pipe problem.'

The Valley of Fear

49. The Warning

The odd one out was EXHOPIN, which, as Holmes pointed out, is an anagram of PHOENIX. The others are anagrams of PELICAN, OSPREY and CORMORANT.

'Ah!' I exclaimed, 'because the phoenix is a mythical bird and the others are real.'

'No, Watson,' he replied. 'Because the others are all birds which eat fish.'

50. The Tragedy of Birlstone

The word is COL, a depression in a mountain chain, many examples of which I had encountered in the frontier war amid the mountains of Afghanistan. Added to the others it creates COLLAPSE, COLOUR, COLLEAGUE and COLLATE.

Holmes was lavish in his praise, as he always was on those rare occasions when I was fortunate enough to pass his little tests.

51. The Scowrers

Holmes pointed out that the key is in squares. 'Any small square of four numbers always totals 22. The missing number therefore has to be 4.'

'These things are always so obvious when one has been

185

told,' I confessed, 'but so difficult to work out beforehand
– at least, for me.'

'Quite so,' replied Sherlock Holmes.

52. The Trapping of Birdy Edwards

The words turned out to be anagrams. Holmes rearranged
them all, and linked them to spell out FOOTBALL,
TEASPOON, APPLE TREE, KILLER WHALE, LAWN-
MOWER, and LIMELIGHT.

I saw it all once he had explained it, though in the time
I could only get TEASPOON, FOOTBALL and APPLE
TREE. My unconvincing excuse was that these were the
only ones I had ever seen.

Reminiscences of Sherlock Holmes

53. Wisteria Lodge

'The second clock will be showing 9.30 p.m.,' explained
my friend. 'The first clock stopped at 8 p.m. in real time;
though having gained 2 and one-quarter minutes per hour
over those 20 hours, it actually showed 8.45 p.m. But that
was 1 and one-half hours ago, so the second clock must
now have moved on 90 minutes, so that it now shows
9.30 p.m.'

54. The Cardboard Box

The answer, as Holmes told me later, is 3 – because any small square of four numbers totals 14.

55. The Red Circle

Holmes got it immediately. The word is MOUSE, making the pairs TIMER and LIMES, BOOED and HOODS, FOULS and HAULS, CASES and HOSED, BEECH and PAEAN.

56. The Bruce-Partington Plans

Holmes had calculated, correctly, that it would be a dead heat, and maintained his eagle-eyed scrutiny of the track without a further word. (Suppose that the original race takes a minute to complete. Then the new engine runs at 200 yards per minute, the old one at only 160 yards per minute. So if, on the second trial, the new engine had to cover 250 yards, it will take 250/200 = 1.25 minutes. In that time the old engine, at its speed of 160 yards per minute, will cover 160 × 1.25 yards, which is 200 yards, the length of the test track. So given the new engine's 50-yard penalty, the two engines will finish the trial exactly together.)

57. The Dying Detective

The connection was simple once it had been explained to me: namely, the first and third letters of each word were the same. Holmes reckoned that anyone with an IQ of 140 – the top 4% of the population – should have been able to solve that puzzle in twelve minutes or less.

58. The Disappearance of Lady Frances Carfax

It proved to be simple enough. The hidden word was LAVENDER. Holmes on this occasion seemed more anxious to have silence for his own thoughts than to set a really difficult question.

59. The Devil's Foot

It took me a little time to work out the third, but then it *was* an overseas trip that Holmes was planning, of course. The items were JUMPER, SHORTS, and (the one which eluded me) CAFTAN.

60. His Last Bow

The answer was 17. 'All the other numbers begin with a T when written in English,' explained Holmes, 'and in fact the ones I have listed here comprise the first fifteen such numbers. Of course, to someone who thinks naturally in German, there is no pattern at all.'

'Because the names of those numbers start with a variety of different letters in that language,' I interjected.

'Quite so. Of course, it is not an easy problem – I would estimate that a person would need to be in the top 1% of the population, with an IQ of 155, to solve it in ten minutes. Nevertheless, on one occasion it certainly did save me from a good deal of danger when an obviously intelligent individual who pretended to be an English gentleman could not solve it no matter how much time he was given. But to someone like you, Watson, as you perceive, the problem presents no difficulty at all.'

The Case Book of Sherlock Holmes

61. The Illustrious Client

Holmes was pulling my leg, so to speak. In fact, the bath would never fill when both taps were running.

62. The Blanched Soldier

It turned out that there were six ways of collecting the correct letters. Holmes later estimated that anyone completing this puzzle successfully in five minutes was probably in the top 10% of the population, with an IQ of 130 or more.

63. The Mazarin Stone

The two missing words were MIRACLE and RECLAIM.

64. The Three Gables

The missing word turned out to be BOOK, making COPY-BOOK, BOOKWORM, SCRAPBOOK, BOOKCASES, HANDBOOK and BOOKMARK.

65. The Sussex Vampire

The missing words were UVULA, NUDES, CLEFT and HASTE. It seems that someone in the top 2% of the population, that is, someone with an IQ rating of 148 or more, should be able to solve this particular puzzle in ten minutes.

66. The Three Garridebs

The missing word is MILL, making GRISTMILL, MILL-POND, WINDMILL, MILLWHEEL, SAWMILL and MILLION. Someone in the top 3% of the population, Holmes went on to explain, would have an IQ of 143 or more.

67. The Problem of Thor Bridge

I hardly dared interrupt my pensive friend when I had found the letter in question. It was T, and the jumbled words were BATHE, DITCH, LATER and METAL.

68. The Creeping Man

The missing word was FORE, making FOREGO, FORE-COURT, FOREWARN, FORETHOUGHT, and FORE-LEG. 'I'm not at all surprised you were able to solve this trifle within the ten minutes I had allotted, Watson,' reported Holmes later. 'It indicates no more than the fact that your IQ rating is 140 or more, putting you in the top 4% of the population.'

69. The Lion's Mane

'Why, I have it right away,' said I as we made our way through the hives. 'The answer is HONEY, and the lines give a clue to each letter of that word.'

'Excellent, Watson! Excellent! And the fact that you found the answer within the time-limit shows that you have an IQ of at least 130, which is in the top 10% of the population.'

70. The Veiled Lodger

It was MARK. The first letter of the animals and places gives the letters of the name, arranged in alphabetical order.

71. Shoscombe Old Place

The answer, as I subsequently calculated, was sixty-eight and three-quarter miles. Holmes congratulated me, with the advice that anyone solving this problem in the ten minutes he gave could fairly claim to be in the top 2% of the intelligence range, with an IQ of 148 or more.

72. The Retired Colourman

The figure I calculated was 57 miles. Each vowel of the place-names is worth 5 and each consonant is worth 7. The totals for each name are added to give the 'distance'. When this is done for the letters in WORCESTER, the sum is 57.